Copyright © 2009 by Bramcost Publications
All rights reserved
Published in the United States of America

This Bramcost Publications edition is an unabridged republication of the rare original work first published in 1937.

www.BramcostPublications.com

ISBN 10: 1-936049-00-7
ISBN 13: 978-1-936049-00-4

Library of Congress Control Number: 2009925321

GERTRUDE MASON'S PATTERN-MAKING BOOK

THE PRINCIPLES OF PATTERN-CUTTING APPLIED TO LINGERIE, BLOUSES, SKIRTS AND SPORTSWEAR

BY

GERTRUDE MASON

AUTHOR OF "TAILORING FOR WOMEN"

INSTRUCTOR OF DRESSMAKING, COATMAKING AND TAILORING AT THE BIRMINGHAM CENTRAL TECHNICAL COLLEGE

(*Lecturer Demonstrator in Needlework, Dressmaking, and Tailoring to classes of Teachers under the Board of Education, The Birmingham Education Committee and the Kent Education Committee.*)

PREFACE

It is hoped that this book will meet the need for reliable guidance in modern pattern-creating, not only of the home-dressmaker but of teachers of needlework and dressmaking also.

For a book of its size much ground has been covered, and the needs of the novice have been specially catered for. It is in fact with her alone in view that the chapter on Simplified Pattern Making has been included, containing as it does details which the experienced needlewoman will find superfluous. On the other hand the principles dealt with in other chapters will enable the experienced worker to develop her own ideas on design, and encourage her to create her own models on the basic pattern types.

The diagrams and instructions throughout the book are clear and simple, so that no matter how drastic the change in fashion, how surprising the new silhouette, or how ancient the revival, and always bearing in mind that pattern making is best learned by practical experience, the woman who has studied the methods explained in this book can with very little practice adapt the mode to her own needs and cultivate her own creative talent.

My thanks are due to Miss Sara J. Turner who has so ably drawn—often, I fear, from very rough sketches and scrappy notes—the illustrations in this book.

Her technical knowledge of the subject has ensured that the diagrams are correct, and that they are rendered in a simple and comprehensive manner.

GERTRUDE MASON.

March 30th, 1937.

CONTENTS

CHAP.		PAGE
I.	THE SELECTION OF PATTERNS	1

HOW TO ACHIEVE ELEGANCE WITHOUT DISCOMFORT—THE TYPE PATTERNS—GOOD TYPE PATTERNS ARE ESSENTIAL—MEASUREMENTS—HOW TO TAKE MEASUREMENTS—MEASUREMENTS REQUIRED FOR THE TYPE PATTERNS—COMMERCIAL OR STOCK SIZE PATTERNS—TO INTERPRET A COMMERCIAL PATTERN—TO INDIVIDUALISE A STOCK SIZE PATTERN—TO ADJUST SHOULDER LINE OF A PATTERN—TO ADJUST NECK LINE OF A PATTERN.

II.	DRAWN TO MEASURE PATTERNS	12

SIMPLIFIED PATTERN MAKING—TO DRAW A PATTERN TO MEASURE—TO DRAW THE PATTERN OF SCARF AND CRAVAT—TO DRAW THE PATTERN OF THE DRESSING WRAPS—A NIGHTGOWN WITH LOOSE SLEEVE BANDS—A TOP FOR SUN-BATHING—A SIMPLE BRASSIERE—FRENCH KNICKERS—PANTIES—COLLARS AND CUFFS—THE CUFF PATTERN—FLARED JABOT.

III.	STRAIGHT TOP (OPERA) TYPE PATTERN ..	26

DRAFT OF A STRAIGHT TOP PETTICOAT—CHEMISE SLIP OR VEST—JUMPER CAMISOLE—ADAPTATION FOR PETTICOAT—ADAPTATION FOR SUN-FROCK—ADAPTATION FOR CAMI-KNICKERS—ADAPTATION FOR PETTICOAT—ADAPTATION FOR NIGHTDRESS—ADAPTATION FOR PANEL PETTICOAT—CAMI-KNICKERS—ADAPTATION FOR BRASSIERE.

IV.	MAGYAR TYPE PATTERN	51

TO DRAFT THE MAGYAR PATTERN—ADAPTATIONS OF MAGYAR PATTERN—ADAPTATION FOR MAGYAR BLOUSES—MAGYAR NIGHTDRESS WITH BUST SLIT—NIGHTDRESS WITH SHOULDER LAPELS—A SHORT SAC COAT—MAGYAR DRESS.

CONTENTS

CHAP.		PAGE
V.	BODICE TYPE PATTERNS	63

CUTTING PATTERNS FROM THE BODICE BLOCK—METHODS OF PROVIDING FULLNESS FOR BUST DEVELOPMENT OR DECORATION ON BODICE BLOCK—CUTTING PATTERNS OF SLEEVES—DRAFT OF SEAM TO SEAM SLEEVE—ADAPTATIONS OF THE SLEEVE PATTERN—SLEEVE WITH FULLNESS AT ELBOW—CUTTING PATTERNS OF COLLARS—METHOD OF CUTTING COLLARS FROM THE BODICE PATTERN—CAPE COLLARS AND CAPELETS—DRAFTED COLLARS : SEMI-FITTING SHIRT BLOUSE COLLAR—ETON COLLAR—STAND COLLAR—COAT FROCK COLLAR—PLAIN NIGHTDRESS—YOKE NIGHTGOWNS—SMOCK OVERALL—DRESSING-GOWNS AND COAT OVERALLS—DRESSING JACKETS—MAGYAR PATTERN WITH SHOULDER SEAM—EMBROIDERED KIMONO—DRESSING-GOWN WITH RAGLAN SLEEVE.

| VI. | A SHAPED ONE-PIECE FOUNDATION .. | 96 |

ADAPTATIONS OF SHAPED ONE-PIECE FOUNDATION PATTERN—PYJAMAS—THE PYJAMA BLOUSE—CROSS-OVER COATEE—A BOLERO—NIGHTDRESS WITH BLOUSE TOP, BISHOP SLEEVE AND ETON COLLAR—SLEEVELESS NIGHTDRESS—SQUARE NECK NIGHTDRESS—STYLE NIGHTDRESS.

| VII. | KNICKER TYPE PATTERN .. .. .. | 114 |

KNICKERS FOR DAY AND EVENING WEAR—KNICKERS WITH FRENCH LEGS—YOKED KNICKERS—PYJAMA TROUSERS CUT FROM KNICKER PATTERN—PYJAMA TROUSERS WITHOUT SIDE FASTENING—CIRCULAR KNICKERS—SKIRT KNICKERS—KNICKERS WITH PLEATS—TROUSER SKIRT.

| VIII. | SKIRT TYPE PATTERN .. .. | 129 |

ADAPTATIONS OF THE SKIRT PATTERN—SKIRT WITH FLARES—A PANEL-PLEATED SKIRT—A SIX-GORED SKIRT—A WAIST OR SKIRT PETTICOAT—SKIRT PETTICOAT—USES OF THE GODET—MODERN COMBINED GARMENTS—ALL-IN-ONE PYJAMAS—PYJAMA NIGHTDRESS—TESTING THE PAPER PATTERN—CUTTING OUT THE PATTERN PAPER IN MATERIAL—PLANNING OUT THE PATTERN—THE CUTTING OUT.

Paper Patterns

I

THE SELECTION OF PATTERNS

TO ACHIEVE ELEGANCE WITHOUT DISCOMFORT

NEARLY every woman has experienced the discomfort of wearing a garment with a badly fitting neck line, or one that is too closely fitting across the bust line, hip line, or upper part of arm, and also, of a brassiere that does not fit closely enough to support the figure. Not only are well-fitted garments the acme of comfort but they will last very much longer. To get that absolutely slick fit that modern fashions demand, a reliable paper pattern possessed of good fit, and style and economy in the use of material is considered a necessity.

THE TYPE PATTERNS

There are five types of patterns:—

1. THE STRAIGHT OR OPERA TOP TYPE

    These are modern style garments of varying length which fit the bust closely and are supported by straps of ribbon, or material, over the shoulders.

2. THE BODICE TYPE WITH SLEEVE

    These fit the neck, shoulder and armhole.

3. THE MAGYAR TYPE

    These are garments hanging loosely from the shoulders usually with no shoulder seam.

4. THE KNICKER TYPE

    These extend from the waist and cover the lower limbs to about the knee, or to the ankle (pyjamas).

5. THE SKIRT TYPE

These fit the waist and the hips, and vary in length according to personal requirements.

Each of these types is dealt with and clearly illustrated in subsequent chapters.

GOOD TYPE PATTERNS ARE ESSENTIAL

They may be :—

1. Bought ready cut in a variety of styles and sizes. These are known as commercial, stock size, or fashion paper patterns.
2. Drawn to personal measures, *i.e.*, drafted patterns.
3. Developed from a basic or foundation pattern, usually termed a " block " which may be either 1 or 2.
4. Cut from an existing garment.

Each of the above methods of pattern construction has some special recommendation and the wise needlewoman will adopt the one which appeals to her, and is most suitable for her purpose.

MEASUREMENTS

Taking measurements is always a fascinating process, and is an essential one in cutting and fitting garments made from patterns. Measurements are of two kinds—*length* and *width*. The length measures are taken down the body at various places, the width measures are taken round. Only half of the front and back patterns are needed, hence only half the width measurements are actually used. (It is much safer to measure in full and halve numerically.)

HOW TO TAKE MEASUREMENTS

It is important that the true waist line of the person who is being measured should be defined, as all measurements are taken to and from the normal waist line. To get this waist line fix a tape securely round the waist and push it well down, when

THE SELECTION OF PATTERNS

it will fall naturally into the proper place and thus give a definite line to measure to and from. The right side of the figure only should be measured unless there is a deformity, when the measurements on both sides should be taken.

MEASUREMENTS REQUIRED FOR THE TYPE PATTERNS

The names of the measurements are almost self-explanatory and for either (a) testing stock size patterns, or (b) drafting patterns to measurements of all types of garments for day and night wear the following will be needed.

1. STRAIGHT TOP OR OPERA TYPE PATTERN

    1. Length of garment : Measured from bust line down underarm line. (Fig. 1.)

    2. Width of bust : Taken round fullest part of figure in front, up under the armpits and straight across the back. (Figs. 1 and 2.)

    3. Width of hips : Taken round the figure 8 to 10 inches below waist line. (Figs. 1 and 2.)

2. MAGYAR TYPE PATTERN

    1. Length of garment from shoulder to hem. (Fig. 1.)

    2. Length of back from nape of neck to bottom of waist tape. (Fig. 2.)

    3. Length of sleeve from neck point along shoulder line.

    4. Width of bust. (See Straight Top Type.)

    5. Width of arm, taken round upper arm near armhole.

3. BODICE TYPE PATTERN

    1. Back length from nape bone to waist line. (Fig. 2.)

    2. Front length from base of throat to waist line. (Fig. 1.)

    3. Back width taken across widest part of back. (Fig. 2.)

Fig. 1   Fig. 2

THE SELECTION OF PATTERNS

4. Bust width taken round fullest part of figure in front, under the arms, and straight across the back. (Figs. 1 and 2.)

Sleeve

1. Length of inner seam taken from armpit to wrist bone. (Fig. 1.)
2. Width of hand, taken as shown. (Fig. 1.)

4. KNICKER TYPE PATTERN

1. Side length for knickers taken from the waist line to the knee in the kneeling position. (Fig. 3.)
2. Side length for pyjamas taken from waist line to ankle in the standing position as indicated for side length of skirt type. (Fig. 2.)
3. Depth of seat (for pyjamas) taken from the waist line to the seat of the chair in the sitting position. (Fig. 4.)
4. Width of thigh taken as shown. (Fig. 4.)
5. Width of bust, taken as previously described. (Figs. 1 and 2.)

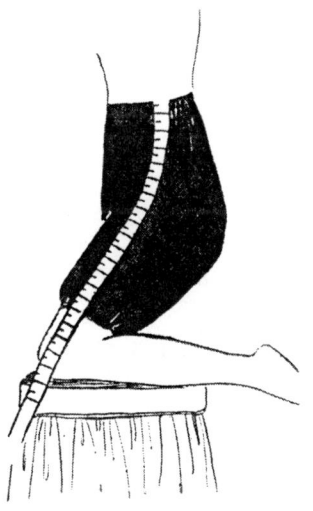

FIG. 3

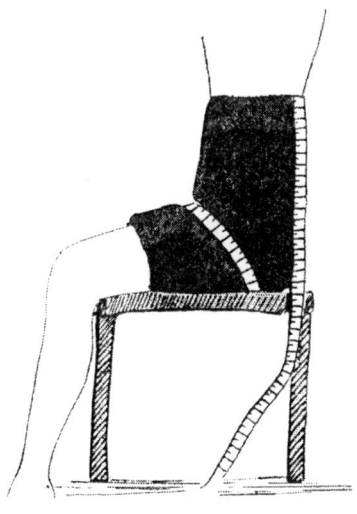

FIG. 4

6. Width of hips, taken loosely 8 inches below waist line.

7. Waist, taken as shown. (Figs. 1 and 2.)

5. SKIRT TYPE

1. Waist measurement, taken easily. (Figs. 1 and 2.)

2. Round hips, taken easily, 8 inches below the waist tape. (Figs. 1 and 2.)

3. Hem width. Varies according to taste and fashion.

4. Front length, taken from the bottom of the waist to the ground. (Fig. 1.)

5. Side length, taken over the right hip (and left if the figure is disproportionate) to the ground. (Fig. 2.)

6. Back length, taken from bottom of waist tape at centre back to the ground. (Fig. 2.)

7. Height from the ground (Fig. 5). Fashion and personal requirements regulate this measure.

NOTE.—It is the height from the ground and the width of the hem that dates a skirt (Fig. 5) not the number of pieces into which it is divided.

FIG. 5

COMMERCIAL OR STOCK SIZE PATTERNS

The most popular method of cutting is by means of commercial patterns. These are sold so cheaply and in such variety nowadays that a great many women who are generally termed "stock size" have no difficulty in getting their garments to fit well. There are a vast number of women, however, who differ in one particular point from stock size measurements. One figure is likely to be broader shouldered or slightly rounder shouldered than another, while lengths of back and arms, and widths of neck, upper arms and thighs also vary. A commercial or stock size pattern cannot be expected to fit all figures alike even though the bust and hip measurements may correspond. Buy a standard make upon which you know you can rely and take the precaution to get the correct size. Ascertain the measurements of bust and hips and buy a pattern to correspond as nearly as possible to the measurements.

TO INTERPRET A COMMERCIAL PATTERN

1. Before opening the pattern see that you have the correct size.

2. Ascertain the quantity and width of material required, also how much contrasting material, or lace, if any.

3. Study pattern—lay-out in order to become familiar with the parts of the pattern and shape of the pieces.

4. Open pattern—replace any part not needed in the envelope, or fashion book.

5. Note seam allowance and how indicated—also hem.

6. Note how the pattern pieces are placed on the material and the indications for darts, tucks, gathers, or pleats.

FIG. 6   FIG. 7

7. Test pattern by trying it up against the figure (Figs. 6 and 7), or by the measurements taken on the figure. The alterations should be made in the pattern and not in the garment after it is cut out. Trying to alter the garment itself is most unsatisfactory.

TO INDIVIDUALISE A COMMERCIAL OR STOCK SIZE PATTERN

Place the parts of the pattern in position according to the instructions with darts, tucks, pleats, gathers, etc., drawn up to size and pin it all on to a sheet of paper.

Test the total length of the pattern, the length of the back, the width of the back and chest, and also the bust and hip measurements, etc. Note on paper how the measurements of the pattern differ from those taken on the figure. It is essential that any adjustment needed must be made without spoiling the balance of the pattern. For this reason unless only a *slight* adjustment of length and width is necessary it is not satisfactory merely to cut wider turnings, or smaller ones as the case may be, as this increases or decreases the pattern the same amount everywhere.

For lengthening, cut through pattern pieces and insert strips of paper as shown (Fig. 8). For shortening, take up pleats in pattern pieces as in Figs. 6 and 7. Make the alterations from armhole to waist line of bodice pieces (Fig. 8A), just below hip level of skirt pieces (Fig. 8B), halfway waist line to fork of knickers pieces (Fig. 9A), and halfway fork to ankle for trouser patterns (Fig. 9B). In long sleeves, 6 inches above wrist and again 8 inches higher. For lengthening or shortening a pattern cut in one from neck to hem, one third of the alteration is made above the waist line and two thirds below it (Fig. 6). The same principles of lengthening and shortening a pattern must be observed for making a pattern wider or narrower. To increase the width of a pattern cut both back and front vertically through the shoulder to waist line or to the

10 GERTRUDE MASON'S PATTERN BOOK

FIG. 8   FIG. 9

hem line and insert a strip of paper. The amount to be inserted depends on the extra allowance needed.

To reduce the width of a pattern, pleat both back and front sections vertically in the same places. The size of the pleats will depend upon the amount of reduction needed.

When the pleating of the pattern causes an irregular or hollow line the pattern line must be straightened or filled in. After inletting paper gradually cut away the surplus edge of paper and so preserve the shape of the pattern.

TO ADJUST THE SHOULDER LINE OF A PATTERN

To make a pattern narrower on the shoulder, take up a dart-like pleat in the shoulder edge as is being made in the Magyar pattern of Fig. 6.

TO ADJUST THE NECK LINE OF A PATTERN

The round neck line of a pattern can be adapted to a square or pointed neck line as indicated by dotted lines (Fig. 8). For a square neck line, measure 2 inches (or depth decided upon) down centre back and front of pattern : then measure straight across the back for 3 inches, and $3\frac{1}{2}$ inches across the front. Rule in the neck line as shown (Fig. 8) and cut out. For a pointed or V neck line measure desired depth down centre front of pattern, then rule to shoulder line (Fig. 8). How to adapt a pattern to obtain a V-shaped neck at the back is clearly shown. Note that the neck line can be lowered on the shoulder as well as at the centre back and front as illustrated on page 55.

II

DRAWN TO MEASURE PATTERNS

INCREASING numbers of women and girls nowadays prefer to make their own patterns than to buy them already cut. They find that the drawn to measure pattern allows for individual irregularities much better than an adapted stock size pattern. Very often the adaptation involves a good deal of time and without some knowledge of the figure and the principles of pattern construction the shape of the different parts is altered thus destroying the proportion which one bears to another and also altering the run of the seams. It is upon these two points that the elusive quality of " good cut " depends.

It should be remembered that drawing patterns to measurements trains both eye and hand to greater accuracy and the eye to a keener appreciation of line, and the connection between patterns and their relation to the figure is elucidated and emphasised. Also, the familiarity with the various parts gained by actually making the pattern often assists considerably in the construction of the garment.

SIMPLIFIED PATTERN MAKING

The garments illustrated in this section were selected not only for the fact that they are dainty and practical, but because the patterns of them include the fundamental principles of pattern making with simple modifications suitable for the beginner. They also give opportunities for the introduction of touches of hand embroidery, edging with bindings, facings, rouleau or lace, and openwork seams.

TO DRAW A PATTERN TO MEASURE

(a) Decide upon the necessary lines on which the pattern is to be built, termed " construction " lines.

(b) Take the appropriate measurements from the body, then

(c) Draw the lines in the pattern freehand.

In drawing patterns to personal measures, the length and width measurements are the primary, or essential measurements as within the rectangle formed by them the pattern is drawn. Only half the pattern is drawn, so all width measures are halved. Before commencing to draft a pattern it is advisable to have the measurements written down for handy reference.

A sheet of cutting out or brown paper, or newspaper will be required, also scissors, a long rule, an inch tape, pencils, and an india-rubber.

TO DRAW THE PATTERN OF SCARF AND CRAVAT (Fig. 10.)

These are easy to make and comfortable and tidy in wear. The ends are slipped through bound, or buttonholed, slits and drawn tight.

Measurements required

1. Length of scarf ... 36 inches (longer if required).
2. Width of scarf ... 6 inches (when folded).

Paper measuring 18 inches long and 12 inches wide will be required for the pattern. Fold paper in half in the length, crease, and then open out. Dot and dash lines (Fig. 10) indicate crease line. For Style A, measure 4 inches to the right along crease line, mark a dot, and then rule from dot to each corner. For Style B, measure 3 inches along crease line, 3 inches at each corner, and then rule shape as in Fig. 10. If scarf is desired narrower at centre back, reduce width 1 inch and shape as shown by dotted line. Note

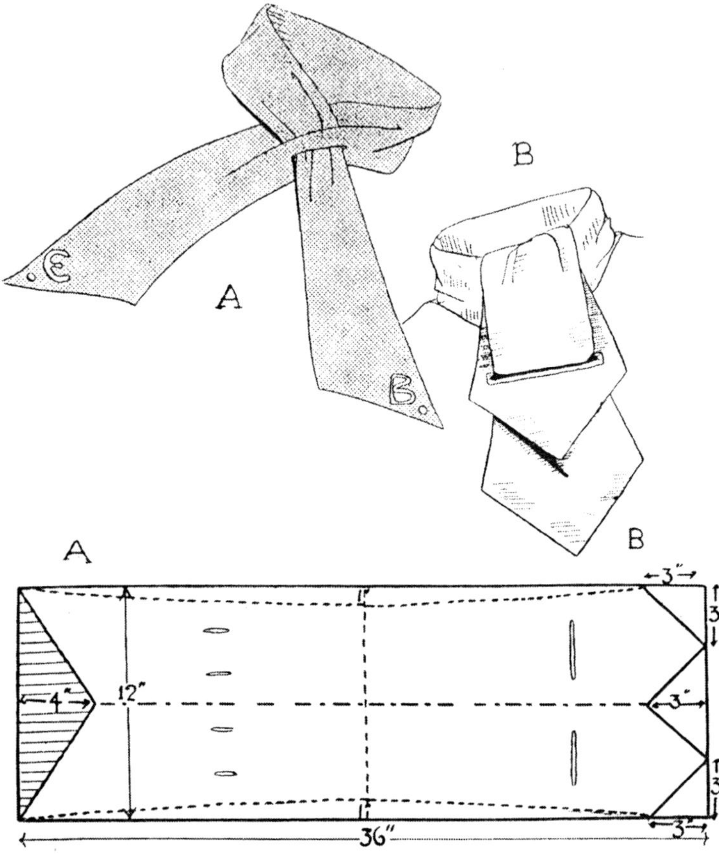

FIG. 10

that the pattern is only half the desired length. To cut out, fold material and place straight edge (centre back) of pattern to the fold. After cutting, open out, and fold scarf in half lengthwise with right sides inside. Machine and turn inside out.

TO DRAW THE PATTERN OF THE DRESSING WRAPS (Fig. 11)

Measurements required:

1. Length of wrap ... ... 50 inches.
2. Width of wrap ... ... 26 inches.

DRAWN TO MEASURE PATTERNS 15

A piece of paper measuring 50 inches long and 26 inches wide will be required for the pattern. Fold the paper in half lengthwise to produce a back and a front section, crease well,

FIG. 11

and then open out. Measure 2 inches from the crease line for the depth of the back neck, 3 inches for the depth of

16 GERTRUDE MASON'S PATTERN BOOK

neck at the front, and 3 inches for the width of the neck at the shoulder (Fig. 12). More or less could be used according to the size of the neck required.

To cut out, fold material and place centre back and centre front edge of pattern to a folded edge of material. Turnings

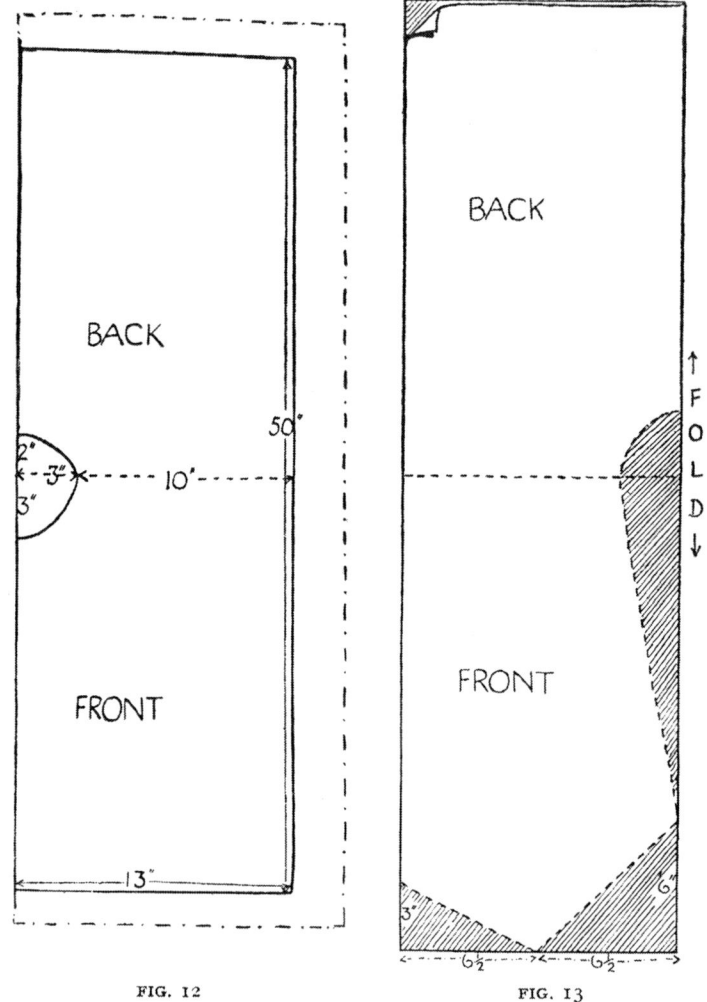

FIG. 12   FIG. 13

DRAWN TO MEASURE PATTERNS 17

are allowed on the pattern. Note that the dressing wrap is open at the front, so cut the material down the centre front fold. The sides are joined by a ribbon sewn to both back and front parts at about 12 inches from the shoulder.

The dot and dash lines of Fig. 12 indicate how to lower the neck line and increase the length and width of the pattern for Dressing Wrap B. Fig. 13 clearly shows the adaptation of the pattern for Dressing Wrap C, and how to place it on material.

FIG. 14

A NIGHTGOWN WITH LOOSE SLEEVE BANDS
(Fig. 14)

This pattern is a development of Fig. 12.

Measurements required:

Length of nightgown from shoulder to hem (Fig. 1, page 4) .. .. 54 inches.

Width of nightgown .. .. .. 1¾ yard to 2 yards.

For garments of this type and length it is usual to draw only a quarter of the pattern so paper measuring 54 inches by 16 inches will be required. Draw lines at right angles for the length and width. Measure 1½ inches down for the depth of the back neck, 9 inches for the depth of the neck at the front and 3 inches for the width of the neck at the shoulder. These measurements may be increased or decreased. Measure down 12 inches at armhole, then measure in 3 inches, and slope side seam. Draw sleeve band as shown (Fig. 15).

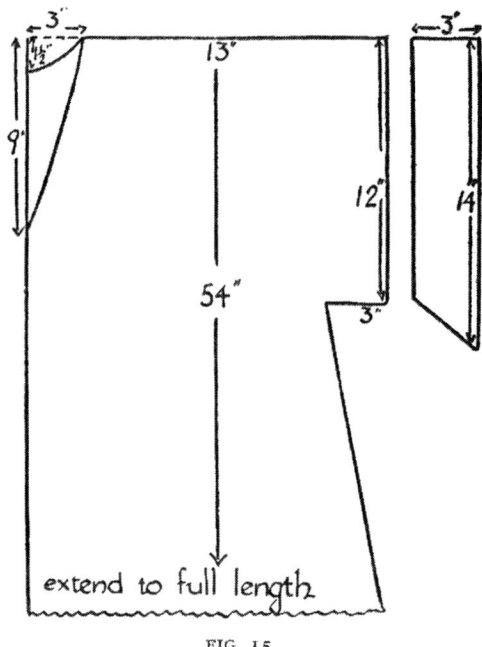

FIG. 15

Quantity of Material required

2¾ yards to 3 yards of 36-inch wide material, or twice the length from shoulder to hem, plus hem allowance.

To cut out

Fold material in half with selvedges even, then fold again with the cut ends even so that there are four thicknesses of the material. Place the shoulder line of the pattern to the fold at the top and the centre to the two lengthway folds. Cut through the four thicknesses for the back neck, then open out material to its full length and cut along the pencil line denoting the front neck and through two thicknesses of

DRAWN TO MEASURE PATTERNS 19

material only. Cut sleeve bands with the short edge of pattern (the width) to the fold.

A TOP FOR SUNBATHING
(Fig. 16)

The pattern is cut from a square of paper measuring 26 inches. Fold paper diagonally, and cut across the diagonal crease line (Fig. 16). Measure 3 inches from the apex of the triangle, and cut where indicated by dotted line (Fig. 16). Fold material and cut out as in diagram. The remaining part of the yard of material required to make the top is cut into strips 4 inches wide, and joined to make a tie

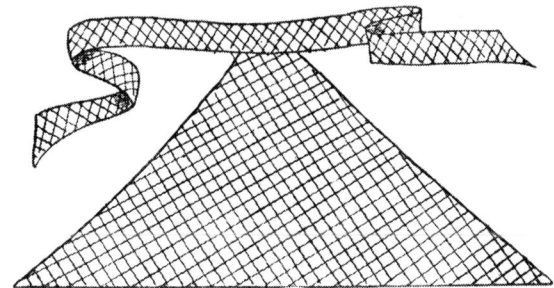

FIG. 16

about 40 inches long. The tie is sewn to the top as sketched. Instead of a tie the collar pattern (Fig. 88, page 78) may be used.

A SIMPLE BRASSIERE (Fig. 17)

The slender lines of dresses with their tendency to fitted bodice effects draw attention to controlling garments which

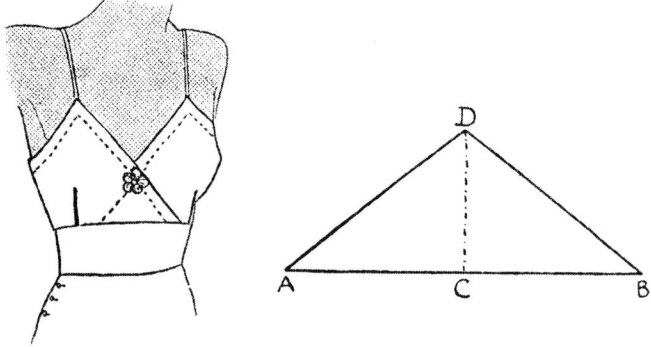

FIG. 17

must be adequate but not rigid. The young girl will find a simple brassiere as illustrated (Fig. 17), sufficient for her lithe figure. It consists of two overlapping triangles of firm washing satin, silk stockinette, or lace lined with strong net. It has no fastening and slips over the head. A piece of elastic joins the two side pieces behind, and ensures a snug fit. To make a pattern for cutting the triangles, rule on a sheet of paper a line measuring half the bust measure, and mark AB. C is midway AB. CD = depth required (6½ inches). Rule DA and DB.

FRENCH KNICKERS (Fig. 11D)
Measurements required:
    Length—waist to fork, taken from waist
        line at back to under chair on which in-
        tended wearer is seated (Fig. 4, page 5),
        plus length of tab   .. .. .. 20 inches.

Width—round thigh (Fig. 4) with allowance
for fullness .. .. 27–30 inches.

To draw the pattern (Fig. 18) paper 20 inches by 30 inches will be required.

Fold width of paper in half and place fold to left-hand side. Measure 1½ inches down centre fold, and 2½ inches to 3 inches from corner and shape front waist line as in diagram. The back waist line is cut straight. For the tab measure 2 inches from the fold and 2 inches up from lower edges of paper. The legs may be left straight or the corners rounded off as in Fig. 18. Cut out the pattern and open out.

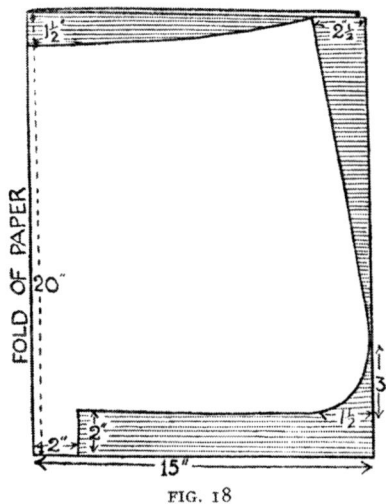

FIG. 18

To Cut Out

Re-fold material and bring the cut edges together. Place the pattern on the material with the tab at the fold. Remember to cut the front waist line through one thickness of material only.

PANTIES (Fig. 19)

Cut a 27-inch square of paper, fold over to form a triangle, then fold again in half and keep the fold to the left-hand side (Fig. 20).

AB = ¼ waist measure plus ½ inch.
C = hip line, 8 inches below A on the fold.
CD = ¼ hip measure plus 1 inch. Rule BD and then cut along this line for side seam of panties.
E = 1 inch from A and curve front waist line EB.
AB = back waist line.

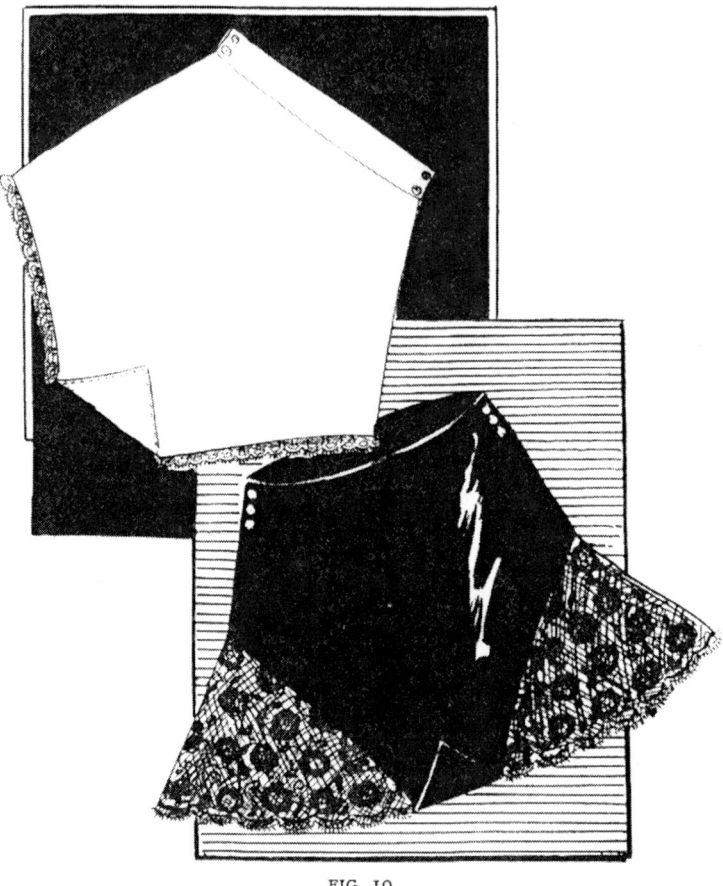

FIG. 19

Fig. 21 shows front and back pattern of panties. The bottom two points are overlapped for the legs, giving the effect of an inserted gusset when sewn one on to the other. Dotted line on Fig. 21 indicates overlapping.

The panties can easily be converted into knickers by faggot stitching the pieces cut off (marked K) on to the slanting legs. Fig. 20 shows the corner section K opened out for the pattern of the godet of lace on the knickers (Fig. 19). See reference to godets on page 139.

COLLARS AND CUFFS (Fig. 22)

A circular collar which can be fastened at centre back or front is shown (Fig. 22). Take paper, crease it as shown (Fig. 23), then open out. The dotted line denotes the shoulder line.

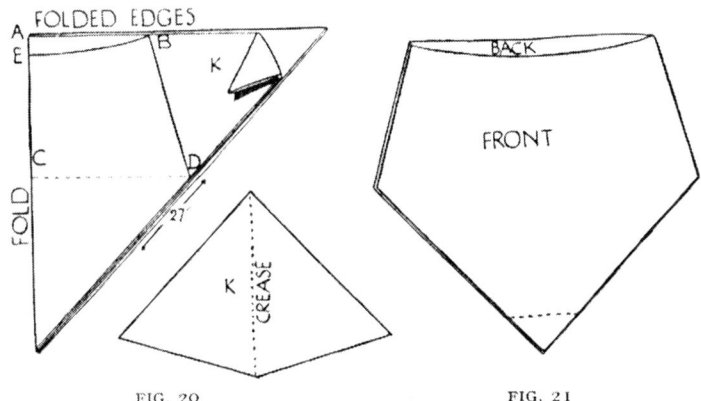

FIG. 20   FIG. 21

A = 1 inch from dotted line. The back neck may be raised or lowered.
B = 2½ inches, the width of the neck line.
C = 3½ inches, the depth of the front neck line. Curve A, B, C. Decide on depth of collar. AD = 5 inches. Draw outer edge of collar parallel with neck edge.

For the second collar make AD 3½ inches and CE about 8 inches. Shape as suggested by dotted line (Fig. 23).

THE CUFF PATTERN (Fig. 24)

Take a piece of paper the depth of required cuff (7 inches) and as long as is needed to go round the arm at the top of the cuff (12 inches). Fold paper in half in the width.

AB is the wrist, hand, or bottom of sleeve measure. Rule from B to top of cuff (Fig. 24).

For the three-cornered cuffs cut as indicated by dotted line (Fig. 24).

24 GERTRUDE MASON'S PATTERN BOOK

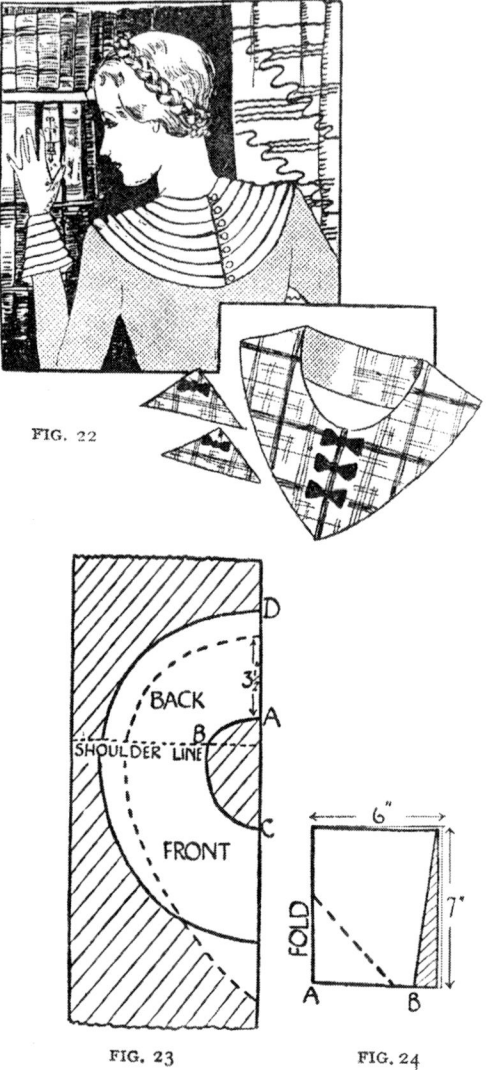

FIG. 22

FIG. 23

FIG. 24

FLARED JABOT (Fig. 25)

The method of obtaining this pattern is clearly shown in the diagram. Cut the jabot and front strap in double material. Stitch inner edges of jabot to straight edges of one strap, and neaten with the second one.

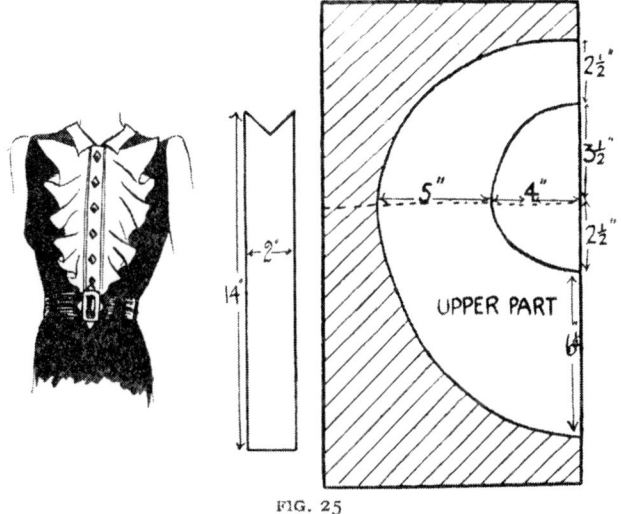

FIG. 25

III

STRAIGHT TOP (OPERA) TYPE PATTERN

CUTTING patterns from a type pattern is the modern method of drafting them and is much simpler and more practical than drawing each pattern independently as described in the previous chapter. The first essential is a type pattern of good shape as otherwise none of the patterns developed from it will be satisfactory.

DRAFT OF A STRAIGHT TOP PETTICOAT (Fig. 26)

Measurements required:

1. Length of petticoat: Measured from bust line down under arm line (37 inches).
2. Length of back: Measured from nape of neck to waist line (15 inches).
3. Width of bust: Taken round fullest part of figure in front, up under the armpits, and straight across the back (36 inches).
4. Width of hips: Taken round the figure at a point 8 inches below the waist line (40 inches).

(See Figs. 1 and 2, page 4, on Taking Measurements.)

To Draft the Pattern

A sheet of paper, long rule, pencils, india-rubber and scissors will be required. Cut paper 14 inches wide, and desired length of petticoat plus 4 inches. Fold the width in half and keep the folded edge to the left-hand side. The paper now measures 39 inches by 14 inches. In the draft the construction and pattern lines are marked in their alphabetical sequence, and in the order in which they should be drawn. The dot registering the measurement is the important mark, the letter is nothing but a name to the dot, and may be placed above, or below it, as may be convenient. Rule a line 2 inches below the top edges of paper for the bust line and mark A at the folded edge (Fig. 26.)

B is the waist line: $7\frac{1}{2}$ inches, or half the back length down from A.

C is the hip line: 8 inches below the waist line.

D is the hem line: 36 inches or required length of petticoat from A.

Rule dotted lines across (Fig. 26).

$AE = \frac{1}{4}$ bust measure plus $\frac{1}{2}$ inch.

$CF = \frac{1}{4}$ hip measure plus $\frac{1}{2}$ inch.

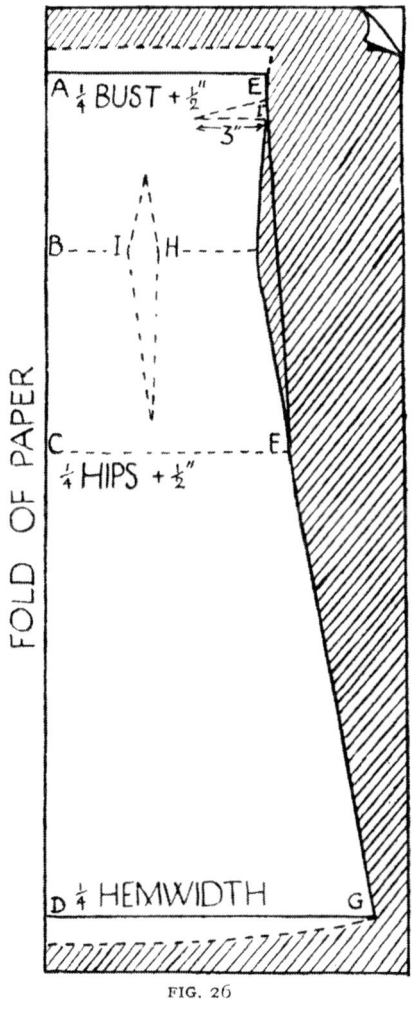

FIG. 26

$DG = \frac{1}{4}$ hem width. Rule a line from E to F and from F to G. Measure in 1 inch or more on the waist line and shape side seam as shown.

The Waist Dart

Find centre of waist line and put a dot. Rule a perpendicular line through the dot 3 to 3½ inches above the waist line and 6 to 6½ inches below the waist line. The need for this dart, and the height and depth of it will vary according to the figure, and the style of the garment, and is adjusted at the first fitting.

HI = width of dart 1 to 1½ inches.

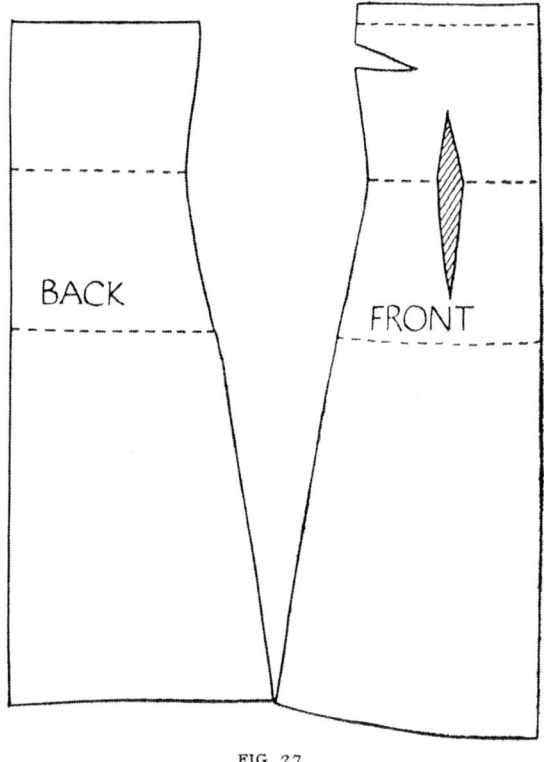

FIG. 27

The Underarm Dart

This dart provides accommodation for the bust and ensures

STRAIGHT TOP (OPERA) TYPE PATTERN 29

a " snug " well-fitting undergarment. Measure 1 inch below E for upper point of dart and 1 inch for the dart. The lower edge of the dart is straight and 3 to 3½ inches long; join to upper point as shown. To provide for the 1-inch dart raise the front bust line 1 inch as shown by dotted line (Fig. 26). Lower centre front line 1 inch as indicated by dotted line at lower edge and complete the pattern.

To Cut Out the Pattern

First trace through to the paper underneath the back bust, waist, hip and hem lines. Cut through the double paper on the side line, the front bust, and hem lines, then cut up the fold, the edges of which now become the centre back and centre front of the pattern. The back and front of the pattern are shown (Fig. 27).

This well-fitting petticoat pattern can be made up in any suitable material, the edges of which may be bound or faced with self or contrasting material or trimmed with net appliqué as shown (Fig. 28).

FIG. 28

CHEMISE SLIP OR VEST (Fig. 28). Adapted from the petticoat pattern.

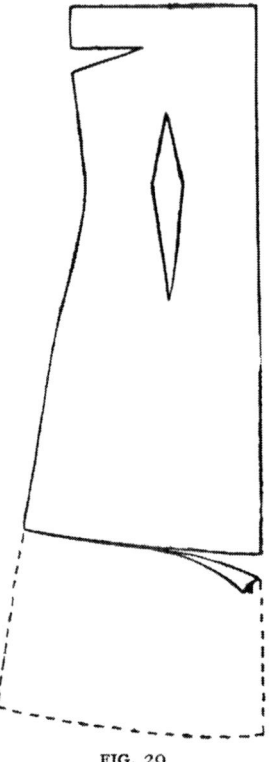

FIG. 29

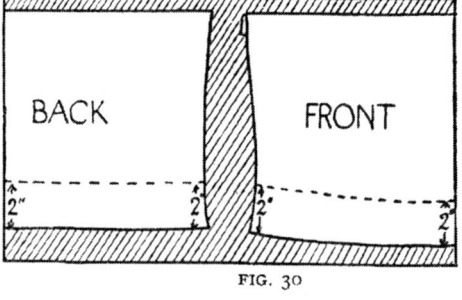

FIG. 30

It will be observed that this is a plainer and more shapely garment than the old-fashioned chemise. It follows the lines of the upper part of the petticoat and is shortened to about 24 inches or 27 inches long, according to the height of the wearer. Sometimes it is worn under the knickers and becomes a chemise vest or " tuck in " chemise. Fig. 29 shows how to shorten the petticoat pattern.

JUMPER CAMISOLE (Fig. 28). Adapted from the petticoat pattern.

This is an occasional garment to be worn under knitted jumpers, and thin or transparent blouses, etc. It is less closely fitting than the chemise vest, or petticoat, so the waist and underarm darts are dispensed with. Take a sheet of paper and place centre back of petticoat pattern to a perpendicular edge and outline the upper part to about 2 inches below the waist line. Pencil in the waist line and remove pattern. Fold down the 1 inch added to the front of the petticoat pattern for the underarm dart (Fig. 30), and place centre front to the other perpendicular edge, and outline similar to the back. Note that the front waist line is lower than the back, usually 1 to 1½ inches. Camisoles may be cut with or without a basque (Fig. 28). If a basque is required, outline pattern 4 inches below the waist line. (See Fig. 111, page 101.)

A Pattern Block

The petticoat pattern of Fig. 26 may also be used as a foundation, or block, for cutting other styles, or garments. One of the fundamental principles of pattern-making is that the shape of a garment depends on the part of the body it is intended to fit. All garments fitting the same part of the body can be cut from one block pattern. Therefore, as the petticoat pattern is intended to be used as a block, or basis pattern, no fancy style features have been introduced. With a little study of designing even on simple lines it is possible to evolve from the pattern any of the modern style features, so that no two garments are exactly of the same design.

Method of Adapting a Block Pattern

Take a piece of paper the length of the garment, and place the centre front and the centre back of the block pattern to a perpendicular edge, then mark all round the edge of the pattern with a dotted line. Remove the block pattern and make the required alterations to the block outline. The adapted pattern will then be cut out along the altered lines.

Fig. 31 shows a variation of the "straight top" petticoat pattern. Place centre front of pattern to a fold of paper and outline. Divide bust line into thirds. Measure two-thirds of the bust measurement from folded edge, and then measure down side seam 2½ to 3 inches according to depth of armhole desired.

ADAPTATION FOR PETTICOAT with shaped flounce, for day or evening wear (Fig. 33).

Place centre front and centre back of petticoat block to a straight edge of paper and outline. Adapt the upper part as described for Fig. 31.

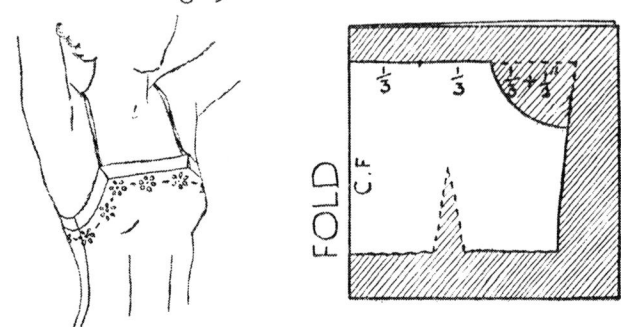

FIG. 31

For evening wear extend the centre front and back to length required as shown for nightdress (Fig. 45). The pattern may be adapted with a low back similar to brassiere (Fig. 54). The added flounce may be of the same material as upper section or of chiffon, georgette or lace.

For the Flounce

Cut off the block pattern at the required depth of the flounce, indicated by dotted line (Fig. 32), and mark the back edge and front edge of the flounce. Cut up from the bottom at intervals (see dotted lines) to ¼ inch of the top. Separate the cut edges 3 inches (more or less according to the required fullness of flounce) and pin on to paper (Fig. 32). Pencil round the slashed section, and then cut out. Treat the back flounce section in the same way. When cutting the flounce in material place the centre back and front to a selvedge fold.

ADAPTATION FOR SUN FROCK (Fig. 34)

This design has a yoke top (Fig. 34A), which will transform it into a smart summer frock. The yoke buttons on to the bodice, back and front. Note that the upper part of the

STRAIGHT TOP (OPERA) TYPE PATTERN

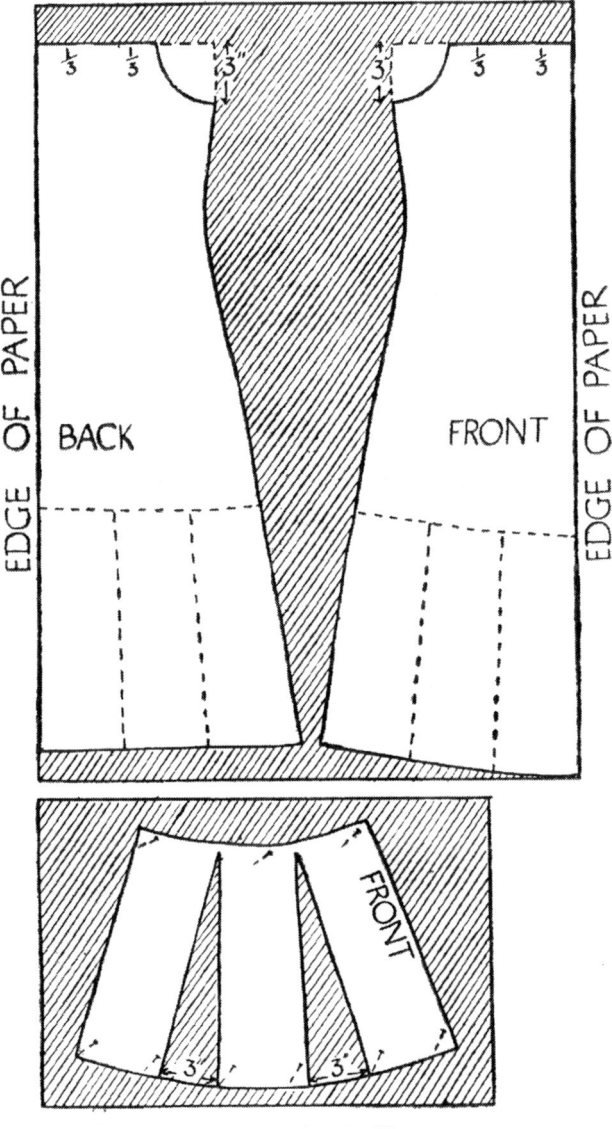

FIG. 32

frock is exactly the same pattern as for Fig. 31, but combined with the skirt of Fig. 145, page 131, and that the yoke top is the same as described for yoked nightdress (Fig. 92, page 83).

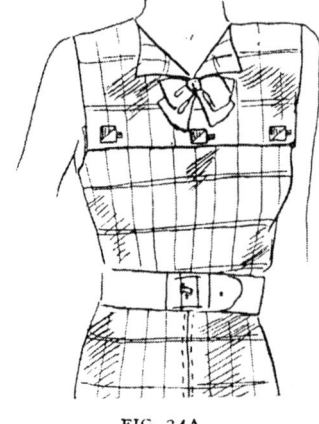

FIG. 34A

ADAPTATION FOR CAMI-KNICKERS

When frocks and suits are so very slim, a one-piece undergarment like the simple cami-knickers design is ideal.

Figs. 35 and 50 illustrate the most up-to-date versions of this practical and popular type of undergarment. It will be observed that they are similar in shape to the chemise vest

FIG. 35

STRAIGHT TOP (OPERA) TYPE PATTERN 35

FIG. 33

FIG. 34

of Fig. 28, and that the knickers part is made by inserting a gusset at centre front and back to button between the legs.

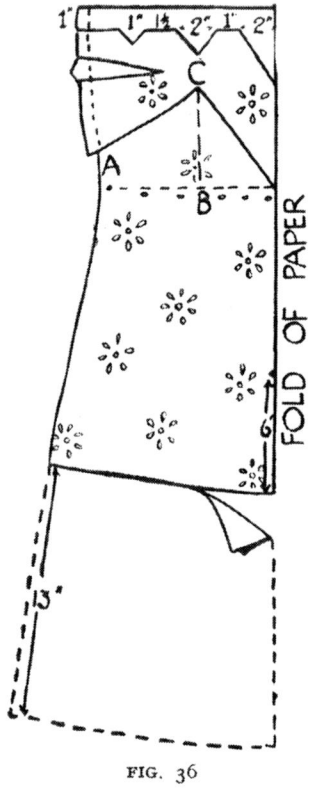

FIG. 36

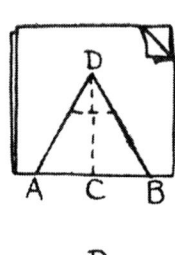

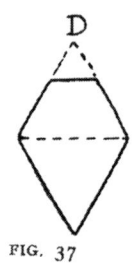

FIG. 37

The style lines are designed to give the necessary uplift and bust accommodation. The lower portion should be cut on the cross of the material to give a sleek fit. *Cami-Knickers* (Fig. 35)

The Pattern

Place centre front of petticoat block to a folded edge of paper, outline and mark in the waist line. Measure desired length of cami-knickers (24 to 26 inches) and cut off remainder of block as illustrated (Fig. 36.)

A = 2 inches above the waist line, front and back.

B = half an inch less than midway waist measure from centre front.

C = 5 inches above B. Widen bust ½ inch and shape as diagram.

Cut out along the style lines from folded edge to C and then to A. Next cut up the fold of paper to produce a back and front section of pattern. Remember to make the

STRAIGHT TOP (OPERA) TYPE PATTERN 37

back bust line one inch lower than the front. Mark a point 6 inches up from lower edge on back and front for insertion of gusset.

FIG. 38

38 GERTRUDE MASON'S PATTERN BOOK

The measurements for the shaped facing which is intended to be cut in plain material, are given in Fig. 36.

Pattern of the Gusset (Fig. 37)

Take paper measuring 12 inches by 8 inches, and fold in half in the length.

AB = 6 inches along the folded edge.

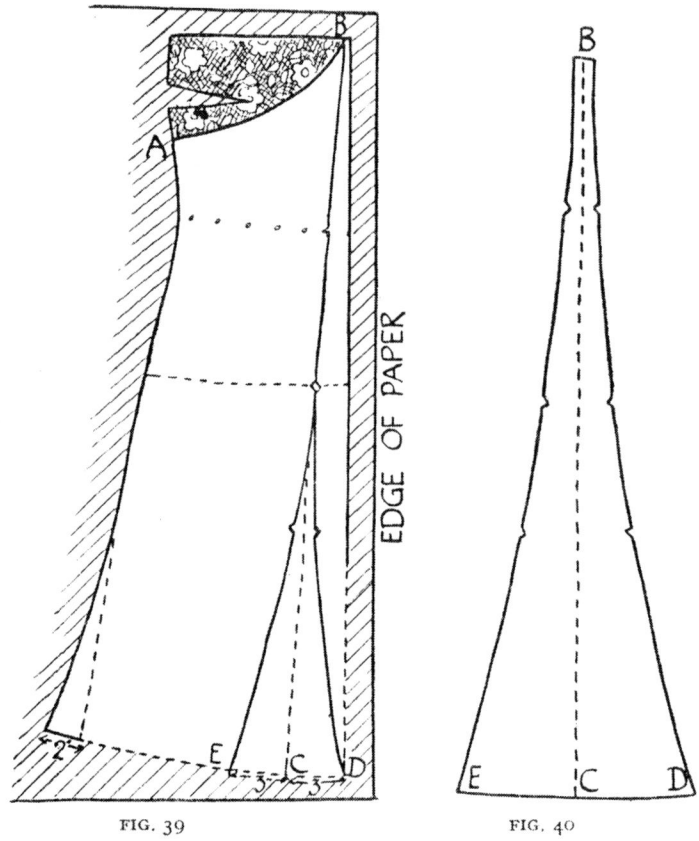

FIG. 39 FIG. 40

C = midway AB.
CD = 5-inch rule DA and DB and cut out. Open out the pattern and cut off 2 inches from point D (Fig. 37).

STRAIGHT TOP (OPERA) TYPE PATTERN 39

ADAPTATION FOR PETTICOAT with brassiere top of lace and shaped front panel (Fig. 38)

The shaped panel of Fig. 38 together with the addition at side seam gives width at hem without increasing width at hip line —a most important factor for modern fashions.

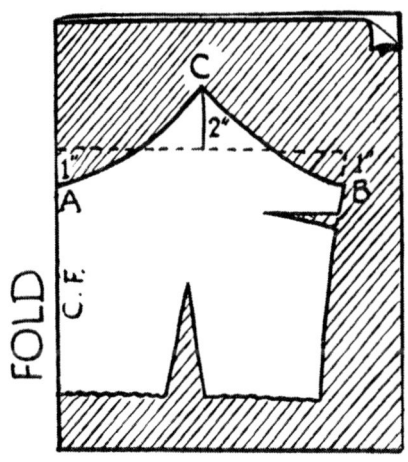

FIG. 41

THE PATTERN (FIG. 39)

Place centre front of block 1½ inches in from edge of paper and outline.

A = 4 inches above waist line on side line.

B = ½ inch from centre front. Connect AB as shown (Fig. 39).

C = 3 inches (or desired width of panel) from centre front at hem line. Rule a dotted line BC.

CD = 3 to 3½ inches.

CE = 3 to 3½ inches.

Shape from BD and BE springing out from the dotted line about 8 inches (more or less) down from the hip line. Add on 2 inches to the side seam, and shape (Fig. 39).

D

40 GERTRUDE MASON'S PATTERN BOOK

The Shaped Panel (Fig. 39)

Take a piece of paper the length of the petticoat, fold it, and place the folded edge to the centre front line of the draft. With a tracing wheel trace off the section BE and put in balance marks (notches) on the waist line, hip line, and 7 inches below the hip line. Cut along the traced lines, and notch the balance marks. Fig. 40 shows the whole of the panel pattern.

Fig. 41 illustrates how the brassiere top is evolved from the straight top. The back may be left straight as drawn, or shaped to match the front (Fig. 41). Place centre front of

FIG. 42

FIG. 43

STRAIGHT TOP (OPERA) TYPE PATTERN 41

petticoat pattern to a fold of paper and outline. Points A and B are 1 inch below bust line. C is midway bust line and 2 inches (or more) up. Shape as diagram.

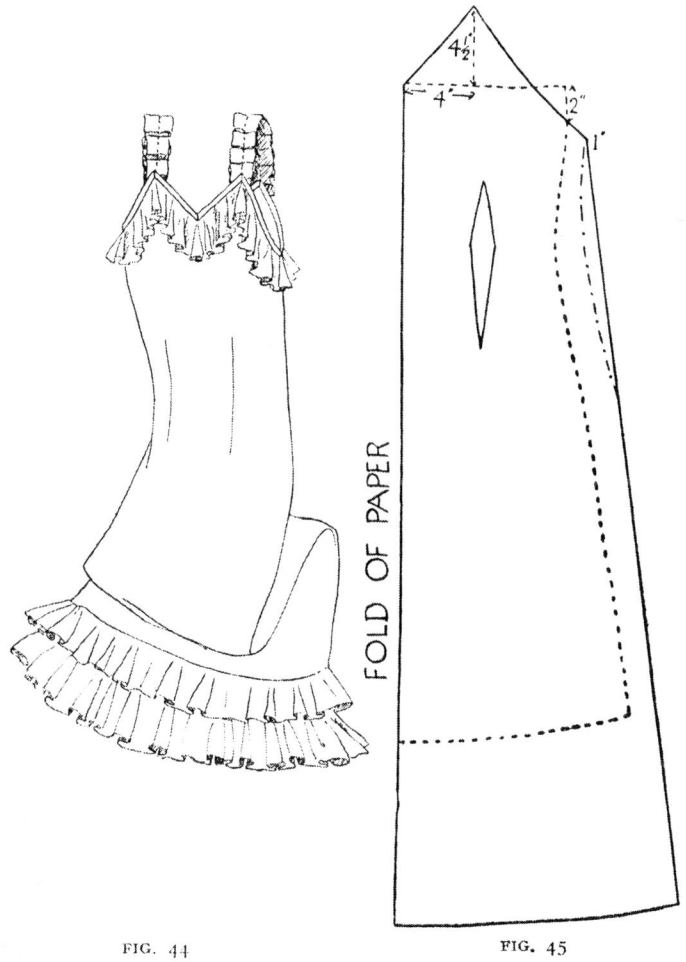

FIG. 44   FIG. 45

The illustration (Fig. 42) shows how the brassiere top may be adapted to the upper part of a sun-suit. The pleated shorts may be arranged according to the directions for cutting pleated knickers, page 125. Use the cape collar pattern (Fig. 86) page 78. The upper part of the pinafore dress (Fig. 43), is very similar in construction to the previous pattern. Any of the dress skirts given in Chapter 8 maybe used in conjunction with this pinafore top.

FIG. 46

ADAPTATION FOR NIGHTDRESS (Fig. 44)

Bedtime fashions become more and more luxurious, and the newest nightdresses are as lovely as evening frocks, with very much the same shaping. Fig. 44 is sleeveless with dainty frills at upper and lower edges and finished with box-pleated ribbon shoulder-straps.

To produce the pattern (Fig. 45), take paper the length of the garment and the required width. Fold paper in half in the width and place centre front line of petticoat block to folded edge, and outline. Extend centre front line to desired

STRAIGHT TOP (OPERA) TYPE PATTERN 43

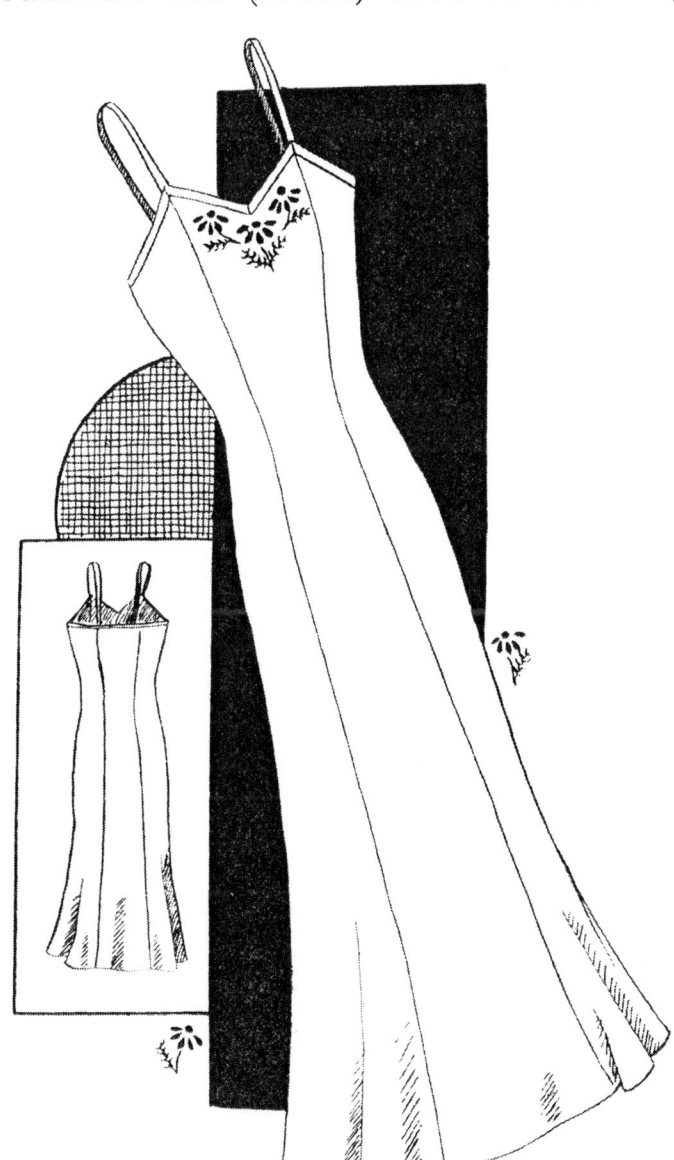

FIG. 47

length of nightgown, and make the width 16 to 17 inches. It is essential that sleeping garments should be loose-fitting, so widen the bust 1 inch and lower armhole line 2 inches. For brassiere style line, measure 4 inches to the right of folded edge, and 4½ inches up. Shape as in diagram. Rule side seam from lowered armhole point to hem line. If a shapely side seam is desired, draw as indicated by dot and dash lines. Compare the upper part of nightdress (Fig. 44) with the evening gowns (Fig. 46). They are similar in design, only more elaborate. Style A has sophisticated straps of plaited lamé. The bodice of Style B is edged with flowers, and has straps of leaves. The transparent cape is cut from an oblong of ninon, tulle or net, and has a draw string of ribbon. A skirt with a flounce (Fig. 32) or godets (Fig. 156), or panels (Figs. 38 and 47) is often attached to a bodice of this kind.

ADAPTATION FOR PANEL PETTICOAT (Fig. 47)

This is a standard type of petticoat, and the hem width may be regulated according to personal taste and fashion. It is an ideal style for a full figure because of its slimming panels, which help to mould the figure.

THE PATTERN (FIG. 48).

Place back and front blocks to perpendicular edges of paper, outline, and mark waist and hip lines.

Back

AB = One-twelfth of the bust measure plus ½ inch, or desired width of panel. Rule perpendicular line from B to hem line. Take out ½ inch on both sides of this line for waist suppression.

D & E = 1½ inches overlap from dotted line.

Shape for back panel from B through waist suppression mark to D. Shape back side piece from B through waist suppression mark to E. Put in balance marks as shown (Fig. 48).

STRAIGHT TOP (OPERA) TYPE PATTERN

Front

AB = One-twelfth of the bust measure, plus ½ inch.

BC = A movable point, about 2½ inches. Rule a perpendicular line from B to hem line. Suppress 1 inch on waist line.

D & E = 1½ inches overlap from dotted line. Widen bust 1 inch to allow for dart at C. Suppress 1 inch at C. Check the lengths of the back panel and side seam from hip line of draft, and make front panel and front side seam the same lengths. Put in balance marks and complete front as shown (Fig. 48).

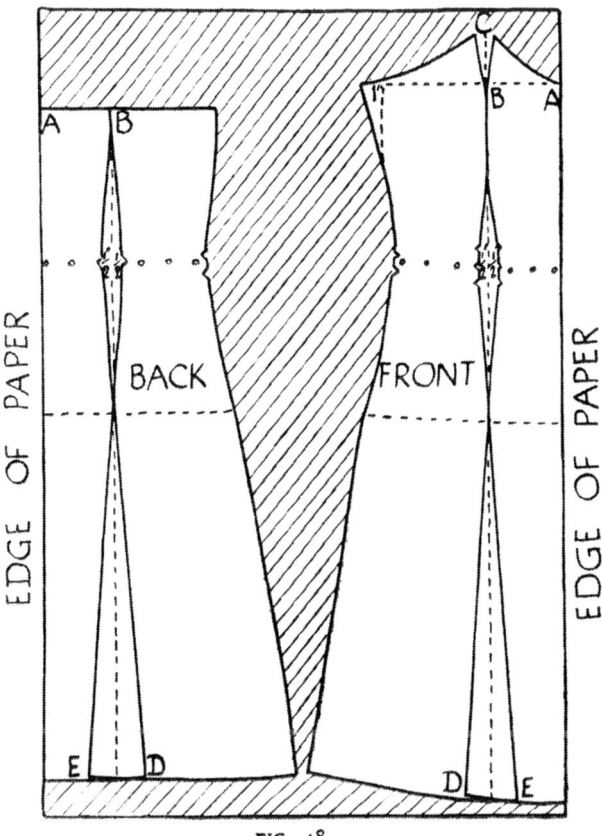

FIG. 48

46 GERTRUDE MASON'S PATTERN BOOK

Tracing the Pattern

Pin the drafting on a sheet of paper, and trace out the back and front panels. Remove the drafting and cut out the panels. Cut out the back and front side pieces on the pencilled lines, and notch all balance marks. The pieces of pattern are shown cut out (Fig. 49).

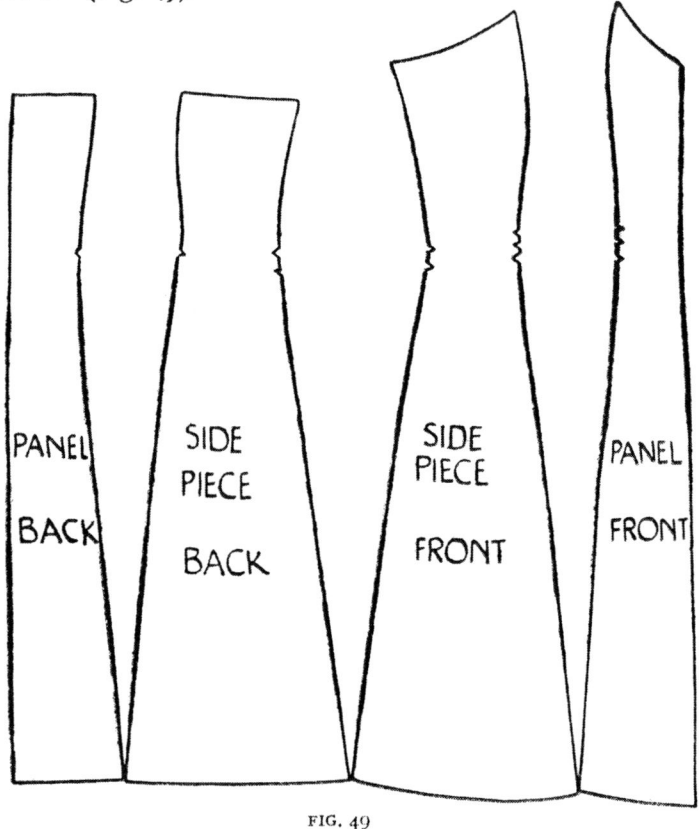

FIG. 49

CAMI-KNICKERS (Fig. 50)
THE PATTERN (FIG. 51)

Place centre back and centre front of petticoat block 2 inches from edges of paper and outline. Measure off desired length of cami-knickers, and mark in the waist line.

STRAIGHT TOP (OPERA) TYPE PATTERN

Back

Lower bust line 1 inch on side seam.

A = 4½ inches (more or less) up from waist line. Measure out 1½ inches at lower edge of centre back and side seam. Suppress a little at centre back waist line and shape as in diagram.

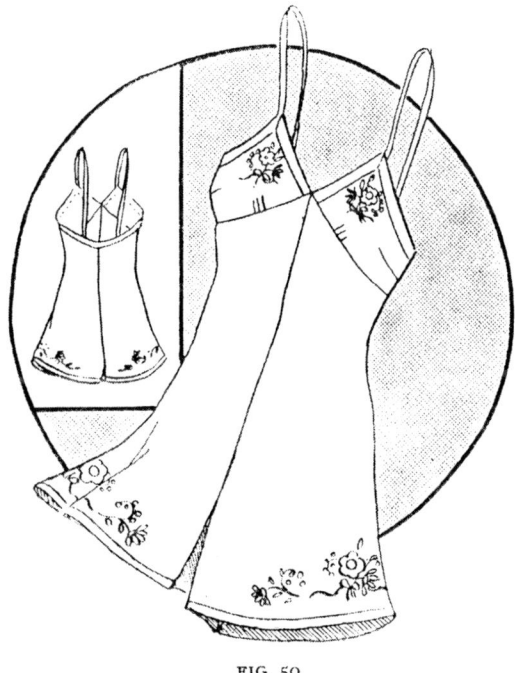

FIG. 50

Front

Lower bust line 1 inch on side seam to meet the back and widen bust ½ inch.

A = 4 to 4½ inches up from waist line.
B = 1½ inches below bust line.
C = 3½ to 4 inches from centre front, and raised 1 inch.

Measure out 1½ inches at lower edge of centre back and side seam and shape as in diagram suppressing dart allowance at centre front waist.

48 GERTRUDE MASON'S PATTERN BOOK

Pattern of Gusset

Take paper measuring 4½ by 10½ inches and fold width in half.

A = 2 inches up on folded edge. Shape as Fig. 52. Pattern of gusset opened out is shown (Fig. 52).

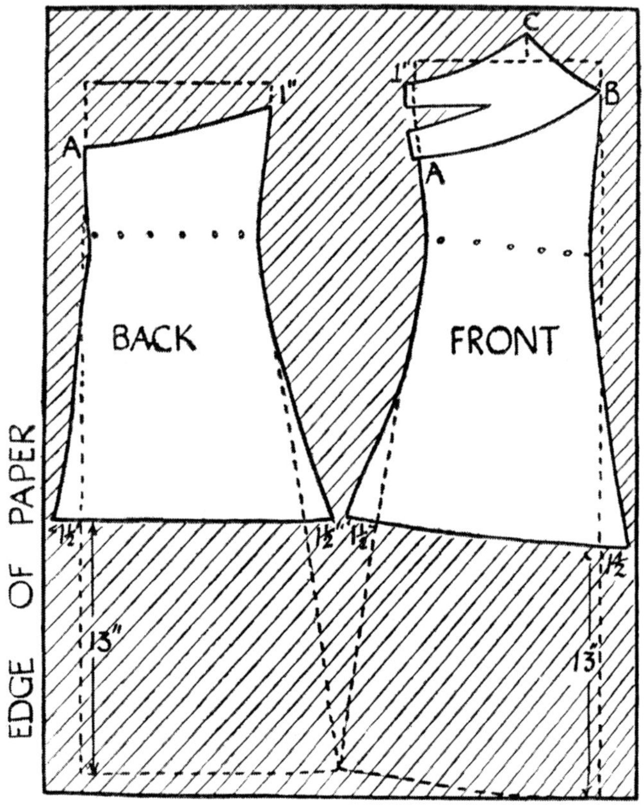

FIG. 51

FIG 52

STRAIGHT TOP (OPERA) TYPE PATTERN 49

ADAPTATION FOR BRASSIERE (Fig. 53)

THE PATTERN, FIG. 54

A perfect fitting brassiere is an indispensable article of attire for the woman of mature figure.

FIG. 53

Fig. 53 has pointed fronts fitted with darts, and a shallow band-like back. It is designed to impart that flat-ribbed moulded effect so essential to the fuller figure.

Place centre back of block to an edge of paper, and centre front 4 inches inside edge of paper, and outline both blocks to waist line, as shown (Fig. 54).

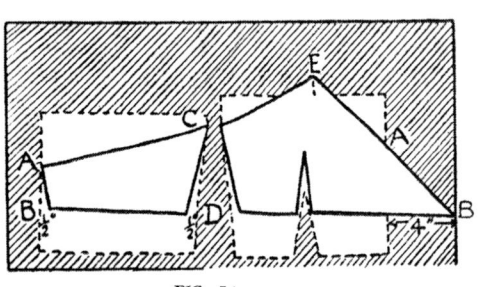

FIG. 54

Back of Brassiere

 A = 3 inches down centre back line of block.
 AB = 2½ inches and ½ inch to the right.
 C = ½ inch below back bust line.
 CD = 5 inches and ½ inch to the left. Shape as in diagram.

Front of Brassiere

 A = 2 inches below front bust line.
 B = 4 inches beyond centre front line.
 CD = CD of back.
 E = A movable point or half an inch less than midway bust line and 1 inch up. Connect EB and complete the front as shown.

IV

MAGYAR TYPE PATTERN

Garments cut on Magyar or Kimono lines hang loosely from the shoulder with no shoulder seam. The shoulder line is extended to form a sleeve. It is a very popular type of pattern for the following reasons :—
1. Its looseness makes it a very comfortable garment.
2. It cuts into a small amount of material.
3. It is simple to cut out and make up.
4. The simplicity of its foundation provides endless opportunities for giving some novel or personal touch in the way of a trimming.

TO DRAFT THE MAGYAR PATTERN (Fig. 55)
Measurements required :
Length

Total length of garment from shoulder to hem (Fig. 1). Length of back from nape bone to waist tape (Fig. 2). Length of sleeve from neck point along shoulder line and down upper part of arm.
Width

Width of back taken across widest part of back (Fig. 2). Width of bust taken round fullest part of figure, in front, up under the armpits, and straight across the back (Figs. 1 and 2). Width of sleeve—varies according to personal requirements.

The pattern is drafted to the measurements given in brackets. Take two large sheets of paper the desired length of nightdress and pin the edges together. The paper is really half the entire length and by using double paper the back and front pattern pieces can be drawn or drafted together. When placing the pattern on material the extended shoulder lines GI are placed together to enable the garment to be cut in one piece without a shoulder seam.

Rule two lines at right angles and mark corner A.

AB = Total length of nightdress (50 to 54 inches).
AC = Back length measure; (15) the waist line.
AD = Half AC measure; (7½) the bust line.
Rule dotted lines across as in Fig 55.
DE = ¼ bust measure, put a dot (9 inches).
EF = 2 inches. Dot a perpendicular line through F as shown in diagram. This dotted line will be referred to as FF^2 line.
AA^2 = ½ inch; the depth of the back neck.
AG = One-sixth of the back width plus ½ inch (2½ inches) the width of the back neck. Curve back neckline A^2G.
A^2H = A^2G plus ½ inch (3 inches); the depth of the front neck.
GI = Sleeve length (14 to 16 inches).
IJ = Sleeve width (7 to 7½ inches).

Put a dot 1½ inches below F and 1½ inches to the right of F. Note the sleeve and bust lines are most important measures in drafting the Magyar pattern. To get a well-shaped underarm curve, and upon this the right balance and grace of the Magyar or kimono largely depends, measure out diagonally from K 1 inch, or more, according to closeness of fit required. If a looser fit is desired move the dot 2 to 2½ inches below F and to the right of F. K would then be approximately 2 inches. The underarm curve is drawn passing through K, and merging imperceptibly into the straight lines of the sleeve and side seams.

BL = ¼ width of desired hem line (16 inches).

Rule from the dot below F to L and shape sleeve seam from J through K merging into the side seam. Add on ½ inch at I and complete sleeve. Make centre front line 1 inch longer than back. Dotted line (Fig. 55) indicates back hem line. Trace off the back neck line and back hem line on to paper underneath. Cut through the double paper on front hem line, side seam, and sleeve lines. Unpin the sheets of paper, and cut back and front neck lines singly.

ADAPTATIONS OF MAGYAR PATTERN

When a pattern has been drafted to personal measures and from which a very satisfactory garment has been made, it is possible, with only a very elementary knowledge of pattern cutting, to evolve from it other styles so that no two garments are exactly the same design. The neck can be V-shaped, or square instead of round, and this style of garment

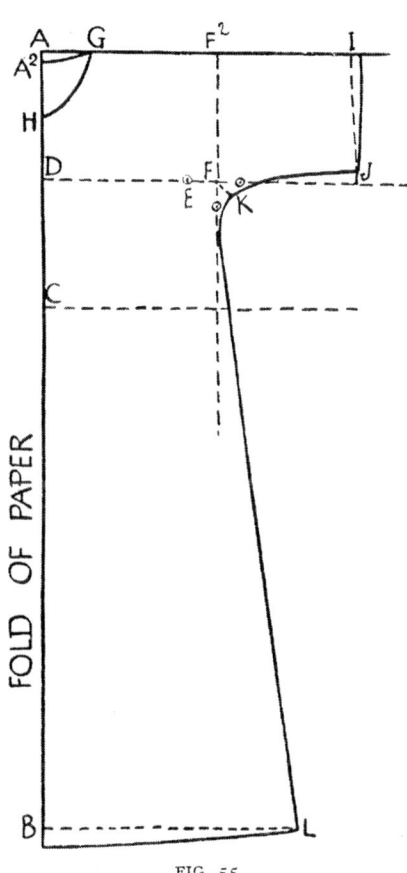

FIG. 55

can well be scalloped round the neck and sleeves. Collar and cuffs can be added if preferred, also a waist sash if it is desirable. Fig. 56 illustrates four dainty and practical nightdresses, marked respectively A, B, C, D; the patterns of which can be quite easily obtained from the Magyar draft (Fig. 55).

54 GERTRUDE MASON'S PATTERN BOOK

STYLE A

Very little alteration of the pattern is required for this nightdress. Lower the front neckline to the desired depth as indicated by dotted line (Fig. 57). Shorten the sleeve pattern by folding up the surplus length as illustrated.

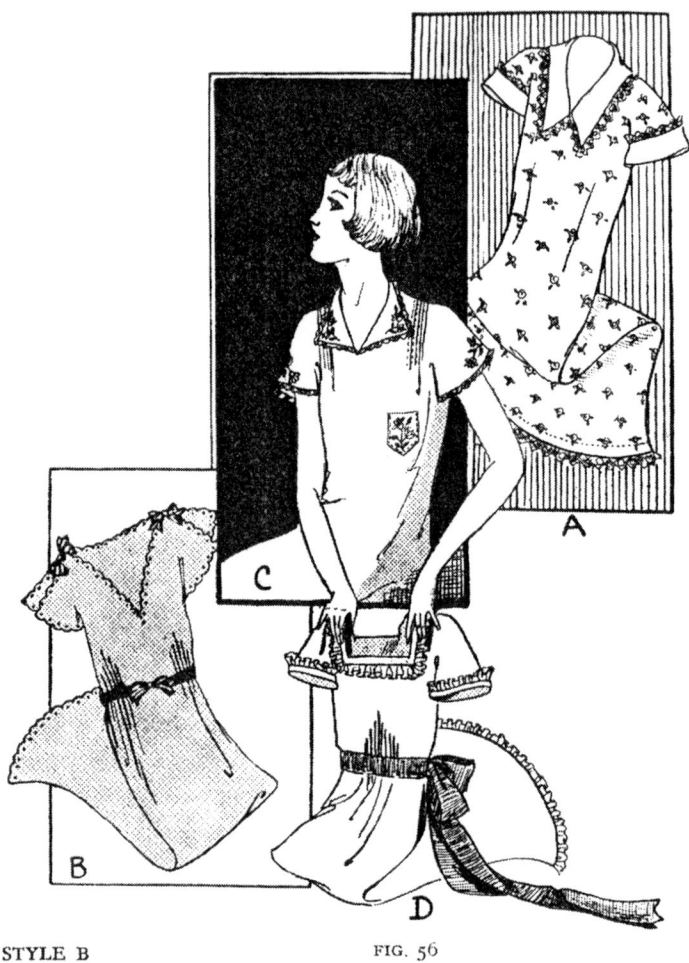

FIG. 56

STYLE B

This nightgown has a sloping shoulder line (left unseamed) and a wider neckline than that of Style A. Lower neckline

MAGYAR TYPE PATTERN

in front to depth required (6½ to 7 inches). Measure ½ to ¾ inch on shoulder line at neck point. Curve in adapted neck line (Fig. 57). Shorten sleeve to desired length, then measure ¾ inch at lower edge of sleeve. Rule in adapted shoulder line as shown by dash lines (Fig. 57).

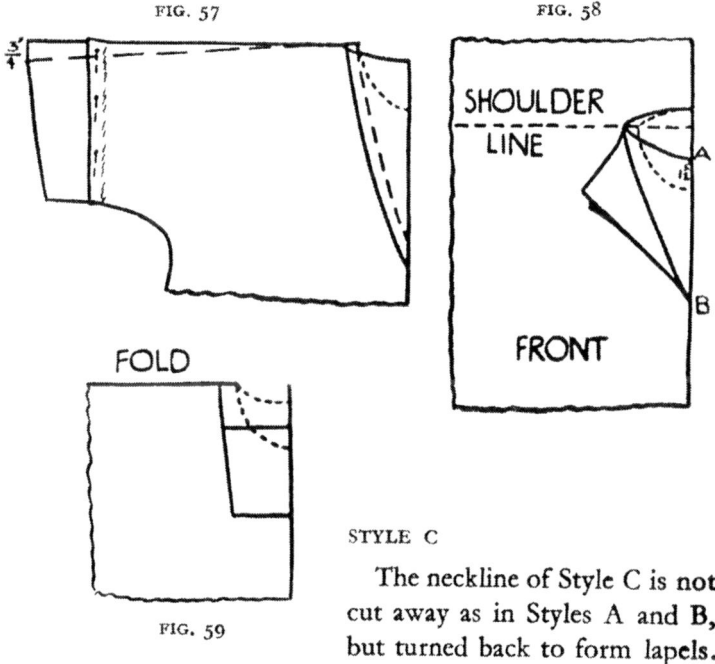

FIG. 57

FIG. 58

FIG. 59

STYLE C

The neckline of Style C is not cut away as in Styles A and B, but turned back to form lapels.

A. Front neckline of pattern raised 1½ inches to prevent point of lapel coming too low on figure.

B. Depth of front opening 5 to 7 inches. Widen neckline on shoulder ¾ inch. Reshape back and front neck lines, and crease back pattern from B to shoulder line (Fig. 58).

STYLE D

Has a square neck line and the method of cutting it is clearly shown (Fig. 59).

ADAPTATION FOR MAGYAR BLOUSES (Fig. 60)

The same principles of adapting the neck and shoulder lines are observed for all Magyar garments. Shorten sleeve as described for nightdress Style A, outline pattern to about 2½ inches below the waist line. Add on a wrap at centre front 1½ to 2 inches. A is a movable point.

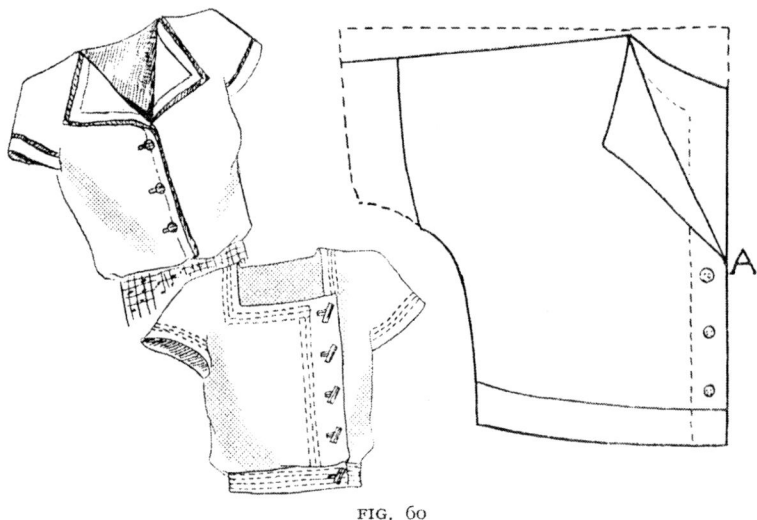

FIG. 60

MAGYAR NIGHTDRESS WITH BUST SLIT (Fig. 61).

It should be observed that the one disadvantage of the Magyar type pattern for adults is that the garment is fairly close-fitting across the bust, and so liable to tear easily under the arms, especially if it is confined round the waist. In the nightgown illustrated (Fig. 61) this difficulty is got over by slashing the front at each side and introducing fullness over the bust. The front skirt is cut of generous width which is honeycombed at each side and sewn under the narrower top part giving a side yoke effect. The fullness may also be gathered or pleated into the slit.

The neck line is attractively finished with a shaped facing,

MAGYAR TYPE PATTERN

the outer edge of which is decorated with stitchery. The short cape-like sleeves are slashed and bound, while the lower edge is faced and decorated to correspond with the neck.

FIG. 61

PATTERN OF NIGHTDRESS, FIG. 62

Place centre back and centre front of Magyar pattern to a perpendicular edge of paper, with shoulder lines meeting.

A = 6 inches from centre front line, or width of panel desired. Rule from A outwards.

58 GERTRUDE MASON'S PATTERN BOOK

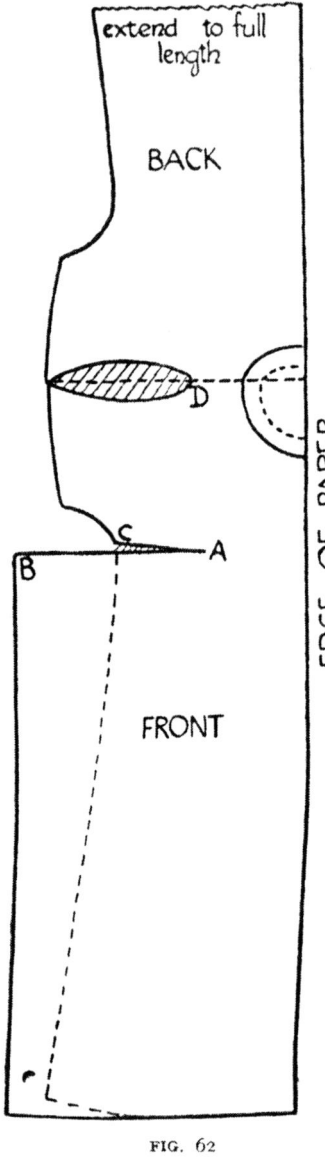

FIG. 62

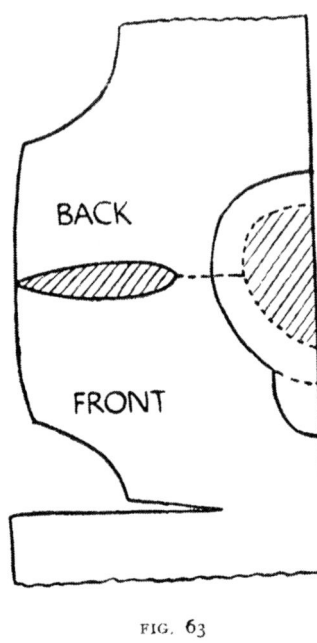

FIG. 63

B = Desired amount of fullness, for honeycombing, pleats, or gauging. Draw line AB, and then from B to hem line.

C = ½ inch. This prevents dropping of side seam. Curve slit CA.

D = 3 inches from neck point on shoulder line. Cut out shape as indicated by shading. Lower neck line 1 inch all round.

MAGYAR TYPE PATTERN

PATTERN OF THE SHAPED FACING, FIG. 63

The facing for the neck edge should be drawn on to the Magyar pattern as indicated (Fig. 63), and to any desired measurement. The outline should then be traced off on to paper underneath, and cut out.

FIG. 64

NIGHTDRESS WITH SHOULDER LAPELS (Fig. 64)
(cut from Magyar pattern)

THE PATTERN, FIG. 65

Outline Magyar pattern on to paper and trace through FF^2 line of pattern. Widen neck 1 inch at shoulder.

Lower front neck line $1\frac{1}{2}$ inches or desired depth. Lower back neck line $2\frac{1}{2}$ inches or desired depth.

A = 3 inches down and $3\frac{1}{2}$ inches to the right of dotted line FF^2.

B = Same measurement as at A.

Shape from A to FF^2 line at front, and B to FF^2 line at back (Fig. 65).

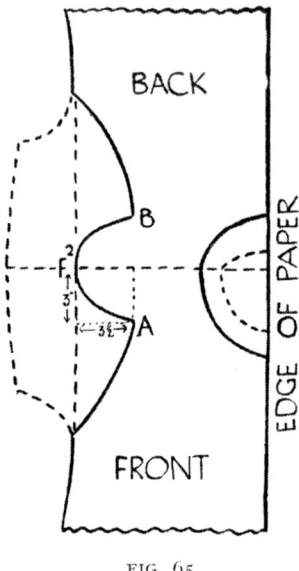

FIG. 65

A SHORT SAC COAT (Fig. 66). (Cut from Magyar pattern)

THE PATTERN

Outline upper part of Magyar foundation pattern as far as the hip line. Add on for pointed lapel as shown in diagram. Make necessary join for long sleeve an ornamental one, by overlapping lower section over upper. Note seam down centre back. Cut a facing to the shape of the front edge of the coat pattern. The skirt is the two-piece pattern (Fig. 144).

MAGYAR DRESS (Fig. 67). (Cut from Magyar pattern)

The simplicity of the Magyar pattern offers endless opportunities for the introduction of modern style lines. The diagram clearly shows how the sleeve line is extended and how the bolero style line is introduced. Contrasting material is used to emphasise the style sleeve. The lower edge of the sleeve may be darted as shown (Fig. 67), or the fullness pleated from wrist to elbow (Fig. 104).

MAGYAR TYPE PATTERN

FIG. 66

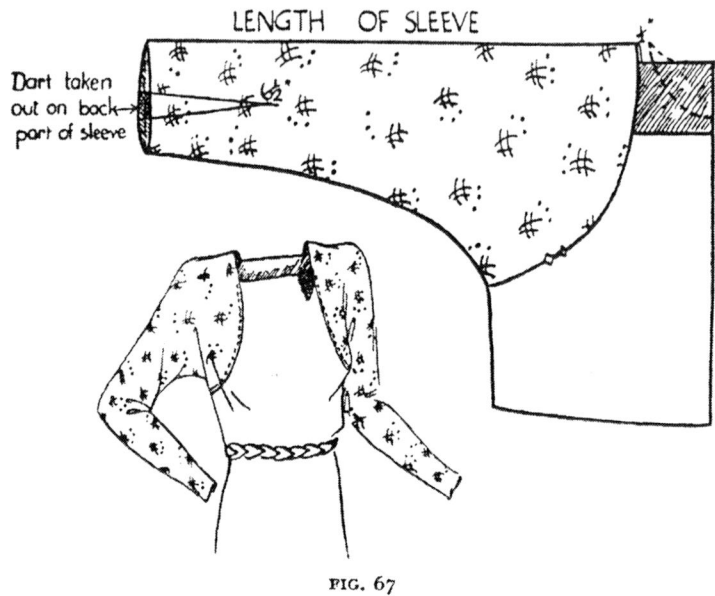

FIG. 67

A pleasing relief from the ordinary style of Magyar dress is the introduction of a contrasting coloured yoke, similar in design to those illustrated on page 82. Sometimes voluminous sleeves are an asset to a Magyar coat, or dress, the sleeve increasing in size to the wrist, there to be pleated, or gathered, into a tight narrow band.

A study of the current fashion magazines will reveal the range of garments it is possible to produce from a Magyar foundation pattern.

V

BODICE TYPE PATTERNS

FIG. 68 shows the foundation pattern or block from which can be cut all garments for day and night wear, other than knickers. It consists of a front and a back which closely follow the lines of the body—neck, shoulder, armhole, underarm and waist line. It is necessary for successful patterns that accurate measurements should be taken on the figure, and as shown in Figs 1 and 2, page 4.

The following measurements are used in order to produce the bodice block for a woman of average size :—

1. Back length. From nape bone to waist line .. .. 15 inches
2. Front length. From base of throat to waist line .. .. $13\frac{1}{2}$,,
3. Back width. Across widest part of back.. 12 ,,
4. Bust width. Round fullest part of figure in front, under arms, and straight across the back .. .. 36 ,,

To Draft the Bodice Block (Fig. 68)

Before commencing to draft it is advisable to have the measurements of the intended wearer written down for handy reference. A sheet of cutting out or brown paper, 26 by 24 inches will be required, also a long rule, an inch tape, pencils, india-rubber and scissors.

Rule a line $1\frac{1}{2}$ inches below top edges of paper. Note the construction and pattern lines are marked in their alphabetical sequence and in the order in which they should be drawn, also that the dot is the important mark, the letter is only a name to the dot.

Construction Lines

AA² = ½ bust measure .. .. .. 18 inches
AB = Back length measure.. .. .. 15 ,,
AC = ½ AB .. .. 7½ ,,
AD = ½ AC, rule dotted lines across Fig. 68.

PATTERN LINES

Back

AE = ⅓ half back width (2 inches) and ½ inch up.
DF = ½ back width (6 inches).
FG = Back neck measure AE (2 inches) measured up from F and ¼ inch to the right.
EG = Back shoulder line.
CH = ¼ bust measure, less ½ inch.

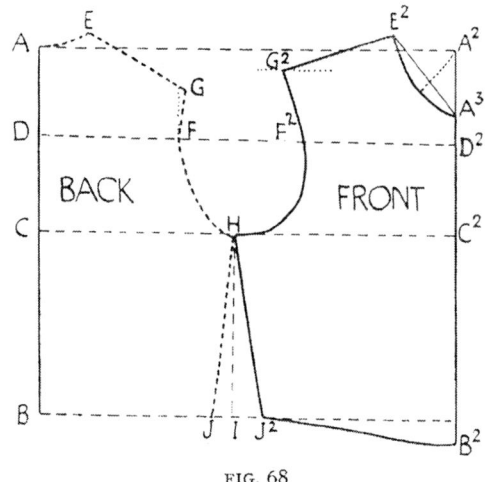

FIG. 68

Curve for back armhole from G, through F and on to H. Rule a dotted line from H to waist line. J = ½ inch to left of dotted line. Complete back block (Fig. 68).

Front

A²E² = Back neck measure AE (2 inches) plus ½ inch and ¾ inch up.
AA³ = Back neck measure (2 inches) plus ¾ inch.

Curve for front neck E^2A^3. Rule a short construction line 1 inch below AA^2 line for the front shoulder slope. Measure back shoulder, EG, and make the front shoulder the same length. $E^2G^2 =$ EG of back shoulder, measured from E^2 to short construction line.

$D^2F^2 = \frac{1}{2}$ back width plus $\frac{1}{2}$ inch ($6\frac{1}{2}$ inches).

Curve for front armhole from G^2, through F^2, and on to H.

$A^3B^2 =$ Front length measure ($13\frac{1}{2}$ inches).

Complete the front block (Fig. 68).

CUTTING PATTERNS FROM THE BODICE BLOCK

It will be observed that the bodice block fits the figure exactly and gives no variety of line to meet circumstances of fashion, or personal preferences. It is, therefore, used mainly as a basis for other patterns. To produce these new patterns certain adaptations of the block will be needed. Since the neck of the bodice pattern fits round the throat the neck line may need lowering, and its depth can be regulated according to the style of the garment, and personal requirements. The neck line also can be adjusted either for a round, a square, or a V neck as desired, as described in chapter 4. In some garments fullness for ease or decoration must be allowed for, and if loose armholes are required the armhole of the block must be lowered. These adjustments need making in pattern after pattern in exactly the same way.

METHODS OF PROVIDING FULLNESS FOR BUST DEVELOPMENT OR DECORATION ON BODICE BLOCK

To provide for underarm dart (Fig. 69A)

This is inserted in the front underarm to provide sufficient ease to keep the bust line smooth and trim. Measure 1 inch below front armhole for upper part of dart and 1 inch (or more) for dart allowance. Square a 4-inch line with underarm line from lower point of dart to centre front line of block. Join to upper point. Lower waist line 1 inch (or dart allowance) at underarm line and draw to centre front.

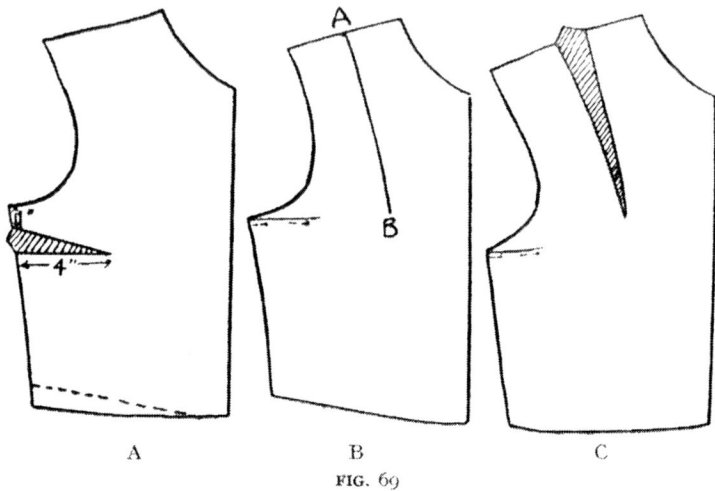

FIG. 69

To provide for shoulder dart (Fig. 69B)

Sometimes the underarm dart is transferred to the shoulder line where it serves much the same purpose. Mark middle of shoulder line A, and rule a line from it about 7 inches long. Pin up the wedge-shaped piece in underarm, and then slash pattern from A to B. Separate cut edges the amount of dart allowance required as shown in shaded section (Fig. 69C).

To provide for tucks or ornamental darts on shoulder (Fig. 70)

Outline front block as far as shoulder point and mark it A, then move point A 2½ to 3 inches (the amount of fullness required for tucks or darts), as indicated by dotted line. Mark the armhole end of the shoulder B, and rule to A for the lengthened shoulder. Outline the remainder of the block with centre front on bias as shown (Fig. 70). Note that this principle of providing fullness or width is applied to the back of bolero (Fig. 67), page 62.

To provide for fullness at front armhole (Fig. 71).

Rule a line for the slash on the front block at the desired position. Usually 4 to 4½ inches down from shoulder and 2½ to 3½ inches long. Extend line 1½ to 2½ inches beyond armhole for required fullness.

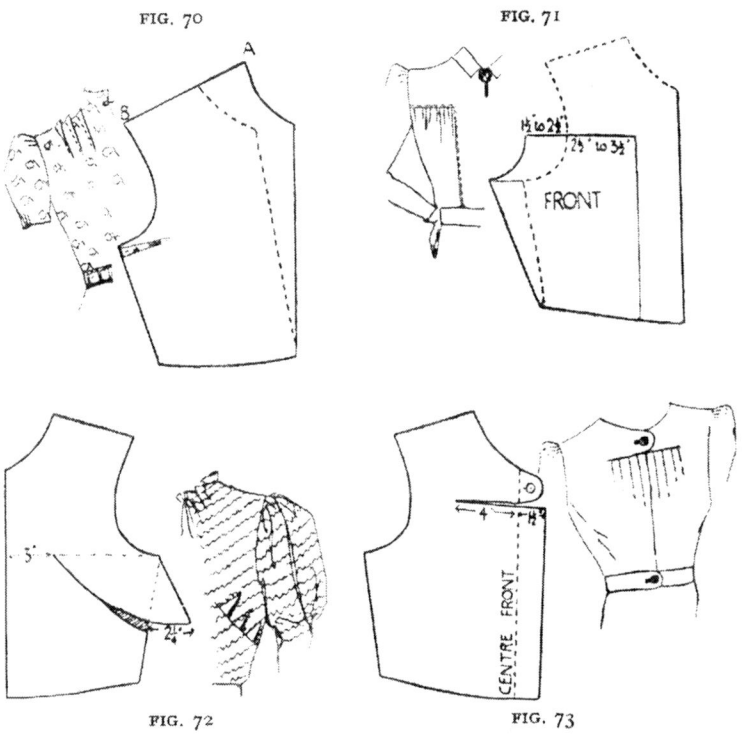

FIG. 70   FIG. 71

FIG. 72   FIG. 73

To provide for slash with ornamental darts at front underarm (Fig. 72)

Outline block on to paper and determine position of upper end of slash. A good measurement is 3 inches in from centre front line on bust line. The lower end of slash is a movable point and depends on its position as a style line. Extend lower end of slash (which is midway underarm length) 2¼ inches for darts. These darts may run in any direction.

To provide for slash with reversed tucks across front of bodice in yoke effect (Fig. 73)

Outline block on to paper, and add a tab as shown beyond centre front line. Determine position of slash and make it about 4 inches long. Extend line 1½ inches (or more) beyond centre front line for tucks (or gathers). Reversed or inverted tucks are ordinary tucks stitched on wrong side. The spaces between must be very even.

CUTTING PATTERNS OF SLEEVES

A modern sleeve draft is based on the circumference of the armhole of the pattern. By taking accurate measurements and with a reliable method of drafting it is possible to obtain a sleeve with just the correct amount of ease and the right balance or hang.

Fig. 74 gives the sleeve block which is often required in connection with the bodice block, and from which any shape can be evolved. It is the seam-to-seam sleeve with the joining seam to the seam of the garment.

DRAFT OF SEAM-TO-SEAM SLEEVE (Fig. 74)

Measurements required:

1. Armhole. The measurement of the armhole of the pattern of the garment into which the sleeve will be inserted. Any alteration to the armhole of the pattern is automatically transferred to the sleeve. Care must be taken with the armhole measure.
2. Front length. The length of the outstretched arm from armpit to wrist line. (Fig. 1, page 4.)

Size of paper required for sleeve draft

The length of the sleeve plus 6 to 7 inches.
The width of the armhole minus 2 inches.

Fold width of paper in half, place fold to left-hand side, and mark corner A.

BODICE TYPE PATTERNS

AB = ½ armhole of pattern minus 1 inch (or less).
BC = ¼ armhole of pattern plus 1 inch.
   Rule a dotted line from A to C.
CD = Front length measure. E midway CD and 1 inch to left. Curve for inner seam from C through E and on to D.
   Rule a dotted line from D to folded edge of paper.
F = 1½ inches below dotted line D. Connect FD.

For Crown of Sleeve

Divide line AC into thirds. G = ½ inch above first third, measured at right angles. H = ¾ inch below second third measured at right angles. Shape for back of sleeve from A through to G and on to C. Shape for front of sleeve from A through H, and on to C. Cut along AGC line, also the inner seam, and the lower curve at FD, and on double paper. Open out and cut CHA line on single paper. This is the sleeve pattern to be used for nightdress, (Fig. 90).

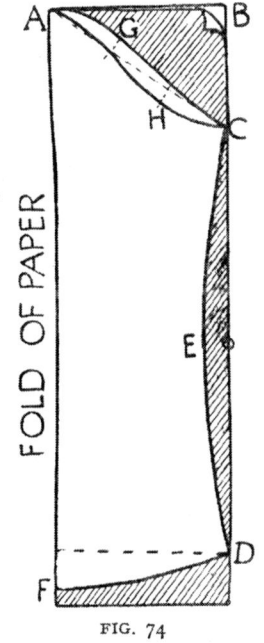

FIG. 74

ADAPTATIONS OF THE SLEEVE PATTERN

The modern style in garment design tends towards detailed cut of sleeves to give style and effect.

For sleeves which are required to be more closely fitting at the wrist than the block, reduce the width of the lower edge at line D of the sleeve draft as shown (Fig. 75), the desired amount.

To increase the width of the lower edge add on at line D 1½ inches or amount of fullness required. This adaptation is shown (Fig. 75A). Re-shape inner seam of sleeve from elbow line and add on a little round as indicated by dot and dash lines. Fig. 75B shows how to adapt the pattern for the short sleeve of yoked nightdress, page 82. Note the ¾ inch of round which is added at lower edge of shortened sleeve.

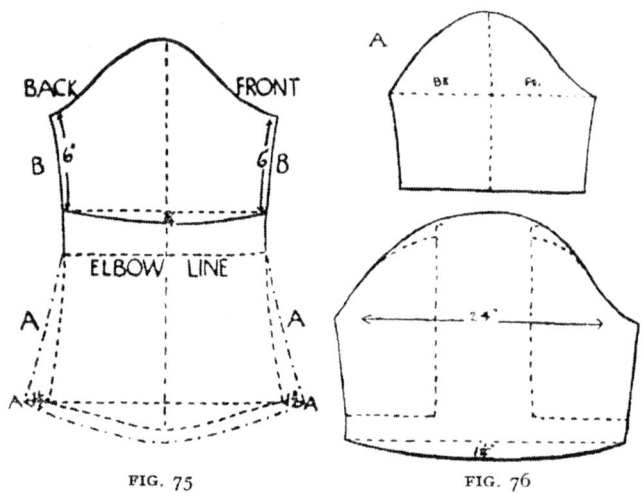

FIG. 75   FIG. 76

PATTERN OF PUFF SLEEVE FOR EMPIRE NIGHTDRESS, FIG. 91

Shorten sleeve pattern to required length (6 inches) and add on ¾ inch of round. Cut up pattern as shown and separate cut edges the amount of fullness required. Pin on to paper and re-draw the sleeve as shown (Fig. 76).

An adaptation of the puff sleeve is shown (Figs. 70 and 72). These puff and pouch types of sleeves are usually made up on to a shorter net or silk foundation cut to the shape of Fig. 76A.

PATTERN OF SHORT SLEEVE WITH FULLNESS AT LOWER EDGE, FIG. 77

Shorten block sleeve to required length (6 inches) and add on ¾ inches of round to lower edge.

Cut up pattern as shown, separate cut edges about 1½ inches, and re-draw sleeve.

BODICE TYPE PATTERNS

PATTERN OF FLARED SLEEVE OF COATEE, FIG. 109

Outline sleeve pattern and mark line D (Fig. 78).

A = 6 inches or depth of flare measured up from line D. Rule a dotted line across (Fig. 78).

B = $\frac{3}{4}$ inch below line A on the fold. Cut the sleeve pattern along line AB. Cut up this section where indicated by dotted lines, then separate the cut edges on to paper until the lower edge is the width required. This principle of increasing width is used for the flared basque of coatee (Fig. 112).

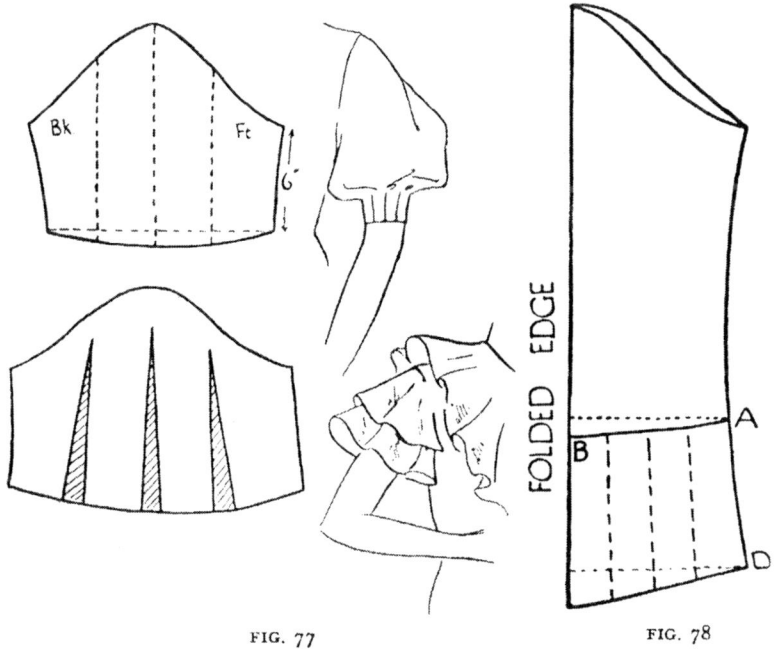

FIG. 77   FIG. 78

PATTERN OF SLEEVE WITH DART, FIG. 79

Outline sleeve on to paper, and mark back and front of sleeve. H-H² midway inner seam length.

A is half-way between E and fold of sleeve.

F

72 GERTRUDE MASON'S PATTERN BOOK

A^2 is 1 inch below elbow line. Measure DE, subtract from this the hand measure, the remainder is the width of the dart measured equally each side the dotted line.

Note both sides of the dart must balance. A pleated frill or a row of buttons add interest to the wrist dart.

Turn-back and gauntlet cuffs often finish the darted sleeve. These may be cut from the cuff pattern (Fig. 24).

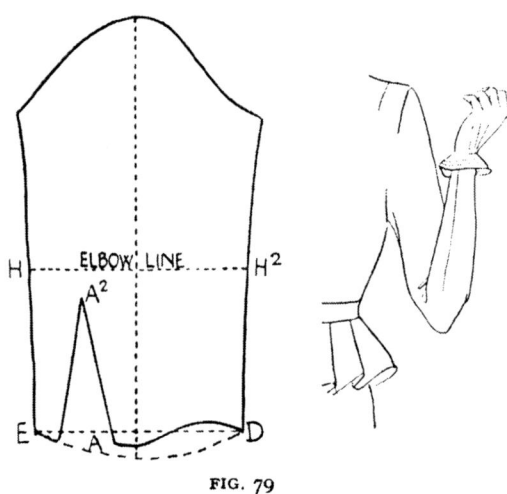

FIG. 79

PATTERN OF SLEEVE WITH FULLNESS AT ELBOW, FIG. 80

H-H^2 midway length of sleeve.

A   =   ½ inch from D.
B   =   ¾ inch below dotted line.
AB   =   hand measure. Shape as shown Fig. 80, reducing width only from below elbow.
C   =   ½ inch.
C^2 =   ½ inch,

SLEEVE WITH FULLNESS AT ELBOW

Complete as diagram (Fig. 80). Run a gathering thread or pleat up the fullness, 2 inches above and below the elbow line on the back edge of the sleeve, and draw up to fit the front edge. Test the correct position of fullness before machining the sleeve.

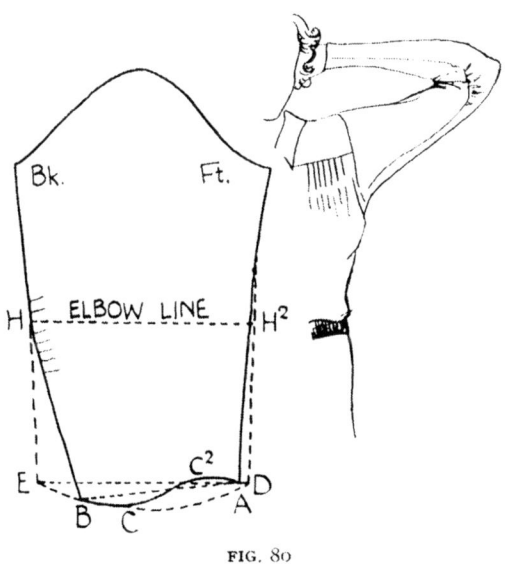

FIG. 80

PATTERN OF SLEEVE WITH FULLNESS AT TOP, FIG. 81

Fig. 81. A shows this fullness gauged into the armhole. At B it is gathered. Note that the sleeve is full and voluminous at the shoulder with a very tight effect down the arm. The sleeve tops may be finished with small pleats or with small darts taken out and seamed. This arrangement produces a squared shoulder effect as shown in Figs. 73, 113 and 161. Sometimes the sleeve fullness is caught in loops or allowed to drape. To produce a loop, cowl, or draped sleeve, draw together points G and H of the draft.

74 GERTRUDE MASON'S PATTERN BOOK

THE PATTERN, FIG. 81

Reduce DE of block to hand measure if lower part of sleeve is required tight fitting as at B.

Measure 6 inches down inner seam of sleeve, and rule line

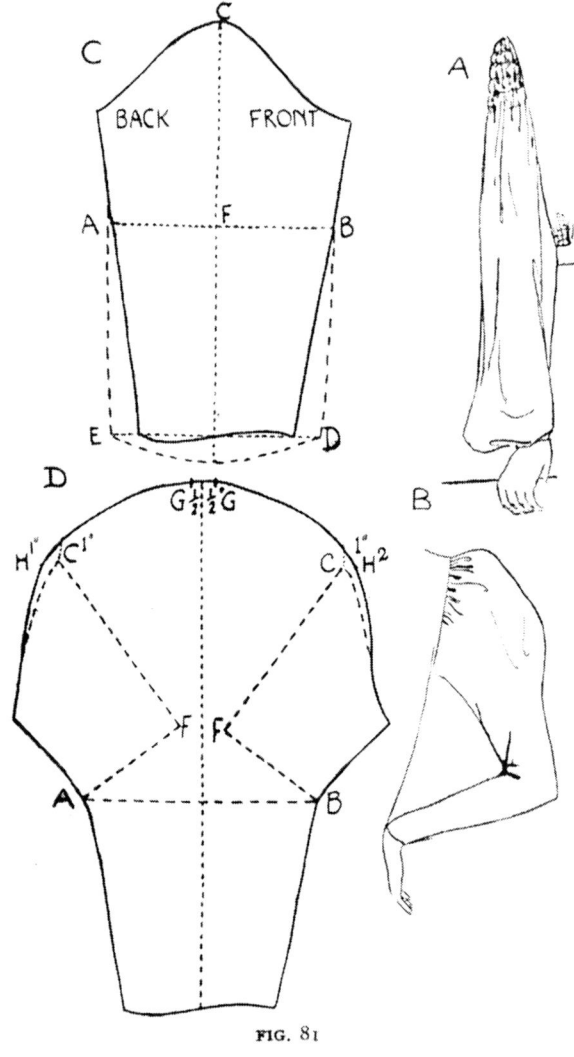

FIG. 81

AB. Cut pattern at line AB of diagram and down from C to F (Fig. 81c). Separate pieces of pattern until CC equals 16 inches (more or less), pin on to paper in this position, place lower part of sleeve to opened out section at line AB, and re-shape inner seam lines of sleeve (Fig. 81D). G = $\frac{1}{2}$ inch. H = 1 inch. Add on 1 inch or more of round at C, and re-draw the top of the sleeve.

CUTTING PATTERNS OF COLLARS

Collar patterns may be drafted, or cut from the bodice pattern.

METHOD OF CUTTING COLLARS FROM THE BODICE PATTERN

Place the shoulder lines of the back and front blocks together at the neck and armhole, and outline on to a sheet of paper. Remove blocks.

Pencil in the shape of the required collar measuring on the actual figure.

1. How far down from the nape the collar is at centre back.
2. How deep the collar is on the shoulder measuring from the neck.
3. How far from the centre front the point or corner of collar is. Measure these amounts on the pattern at the corresponding points, and draw in the shapes.

Collar of nightdress (Fig. 90)
Method (Fig. 82)

Place back and front of nightdress pattern together on to paper, with shoulder lines meeting, and outline the upper part of back and front. *Note*—Both the adapted neck line and the block line are shown in Fig. 82. Measure down 3 inches at centre back, 3 inches at the shoulders, and 4½ to 6 inches at centre front. Measure out 1 inch from centre front for points of the collar, and complete as Fig. 82.

Roll over collars from bodice block (Figs. 83 and 84)

Collars that lie close to the garment, but roll over at the neck instead of fitting flat as illustrated on Fig. 90 may be cut from the block.

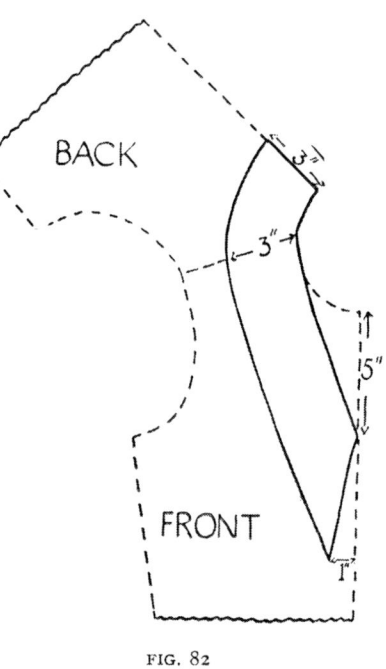

FIG. 82

Collar of Dressing-gown (Fig. 100)
Method (Fig. 83)

Place the back and front of the dressing-gown pattern together on to paper with the shoulder lines meeting at the neck but overlapping one inch at the armhole. Outline in this position and remove the pattern. Measure down 2 inches at centre back, 2 inches on the shoulder, and then sketch in the shape as shown (Fig. 83).

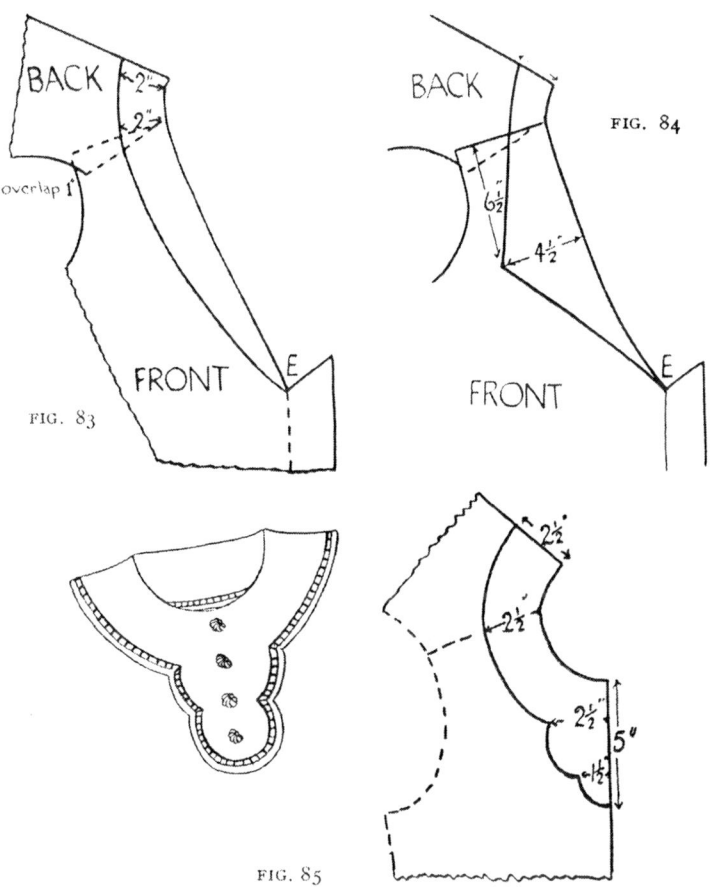

FIG. 83
FIG. 84
FIG. 85

Collar of Dressing-gown (Fig. 101)

The method of obtaining this style of collar is clearly shown in Fig. 84.

A very satisfactory roll collar may be made as follows. Cut a strip of crossway material the neck line of garment in length, and 6 to 7 inches wide (3 to 3½ inches on double). Shape ends off to centre of strip either end, then stretch the fold at these ends to allow slight shaping. The method of obtaining a fancy type of collar is shown (Fig. 85).

CAPE COLLARS AND CAPELETS (Fig. 86)

Method

Take the back and front sections of the bodice pattern and place them on to paper with the shoulder lines meeting at the armhole, but separated for 1½ to 2 inches at the neck line as clearly shown (Fig. 86). Measure down the centre back line the desired depth of cape, 8 to 12 inches. Measure the same amount at the front, and 2 to 3 inches longer at the shoulder line. Measure back from the centre front 1½ to 2 inches, then pencil in the desired shape and cut out.

DRAFTED COLLARS
SEMI-FITTING SHIRT BLOUSE COLLAR (Fig. 87)

AB = half neck measure of pattern.

AC = desired depth of collar (3 inches) plus ½ inch (3½ inches). Rule rectangle and letter corners as shown.

AE = ½ inch. Curve EB. This is the neck edge of collar.

DF = 2¼ inches. Rule FB.

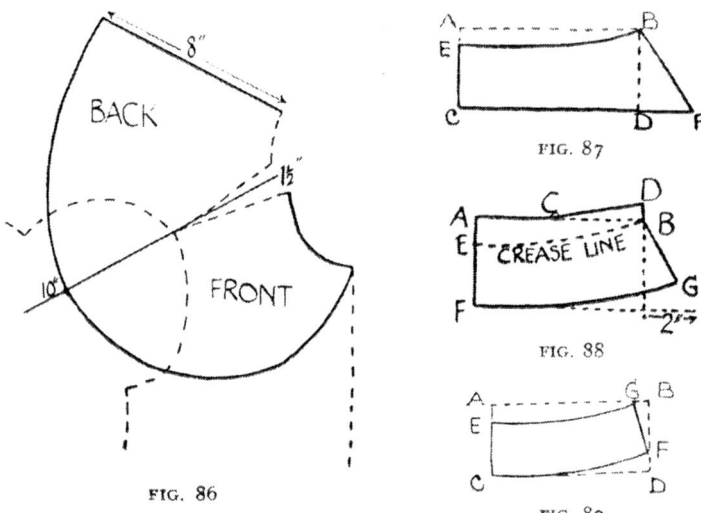

FIG. 86

FIG. 87

FIG. 88

FIG. 89

BODICE TYPE PATTERNS

ETON COLLAR (Fig. 88)

This is a one-piece turn down collar, over a stand, cut away in front. The style of the front may vary. The line that divides the stand from the fall is known as the crease line.

Draw two lines at right angles and letter the corner A.

AB = half neck measure of garment.
C = midway AB.
D = ¾ inch above B.
  Shape neck edge of collar from A through C and on to D.
AE = 1 inch, or desired depth of stand.
  Curve EB.
EF = 2¼ to 2½ inches, or desired depth of fall.
  Rule a dotted line from F 2 inches (more or less) longer than line AB (Fig. 88). Make BG ¼ to ½ inch longer than EF.

STAND COLLAR (Fig. 89)

Measurements
1. Lower neck measure.
2. Upper neck measure.
3. Depth desired.

AB = half lower neck measure.
AC = depth of collar plus 1 inch.
AE = 1 inch.
DF = 1 inch.
AG = half upper neck measure.

COAT-FROCK COLLAR. Illustrated (Fig. 106, page **94**)

AB = half the neck measure of garment from centre back to within 2 inches of end of lapel.
AC = depth of collar (3 inches). Rule in the rectangle.
BE = the collar end—¼ inch less than the closed edge of lapel (1¾ inches) and ½ inch to the right.
  Complete collar as shown (Fig. 106, page **94**).

80 GERTRUDE MASON'S PATTERN BOOK

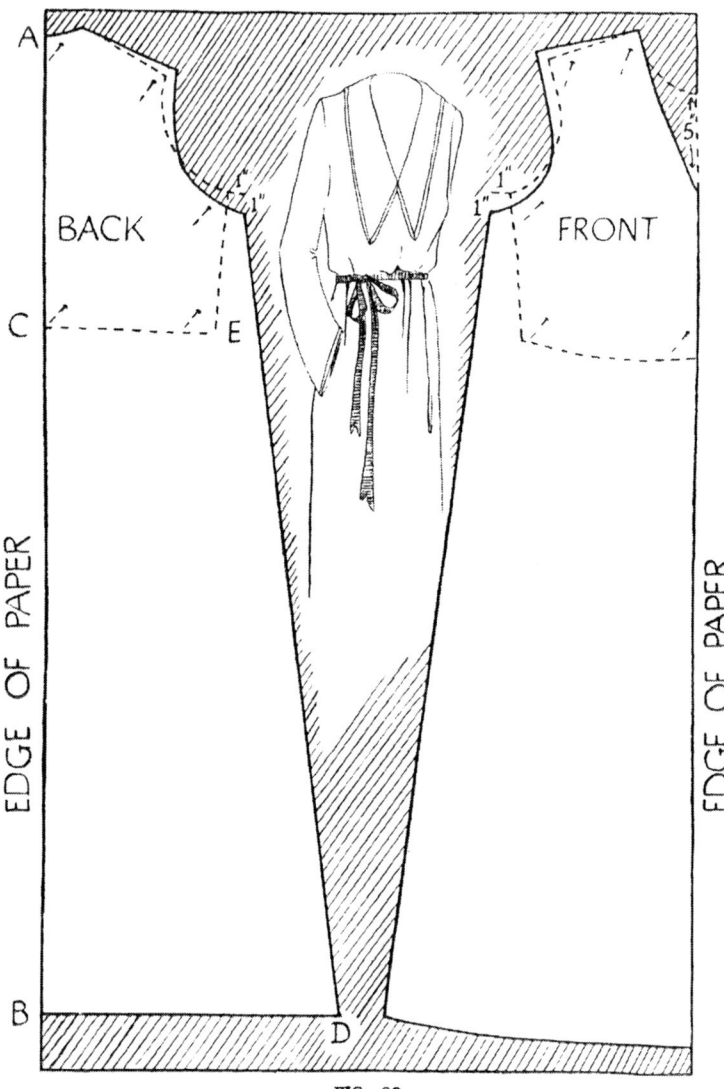

FIG. 90

PLAIN NIGHTDRESS, with long sleeves and collar (Fig. 90). (Cut from bodice block.)

It is essential that garments intended for nightwear should be loose fitting to give ease and comfort when worn. The following additions are usually made to the block pattern when adapting garments for bedroom and nightwear.

Shoulder: Lengthened ½ inch. Raised ½ inch at shoulder point.

Armhole: Lowered 1 inch for garments with sleeves. Lowered ½ inch for sleeveless garments.

Bust: Widened ½ inch, or 1 inch at armhole side to give required ease, and to prevent garment tearing under the arm.

THE PATTERN, FIG. 90

Procure paper the length of the garment. Place back and front bodice blocks, with centre front, and centre back lines touching the perpendicular edges of paper. Pencil all round each block with a dotted line, and then remove the blocks (Fig. 90). Raise shoulder points ½ inch, lengthen shoulders ½ inch. Widen bust 1 inch. Lower armholes 1 inch, re-shape as shown (Fig. 90). Extend centre back line of block to desired length of nightdress.

Back

AB = total length of nightdress.

CB = additional length from waist line; make a note of this length.

BD = 16½ to 17½ inches, or ¼ total width of bottom edge. (This width varies according to personal taste and fashion; the back and front are usually the same width.) Rule from D to underarm point, and make ED equal CB in length.

Front

Measure additional length CB from the waist line. Make hem width the same as back. Rule in front underarm line which should be the same length as back underarm line.

Lower front neck 5 inches, or desired depth. Shape front neck, and cut out the nightdress pattern along the altered lines of the block.

For pattern of sleeve, see Fig. 74, page 69.

82 GERTRUDE MASON'S PATTERN BOOK

YOKE NIGHTGOWNS cut from bodice block.

In Fig. 91 are shown four nightgowns with yokes marked respectively A, B, C, D, all of which can be evolved from the bodice pattern as will be seen clearly in the following diagrams.

FIG. 91

Nightgown A has a deep yoke at back and front with a seam on the shoulders.

To cut Yoke A (Fig. 92)

Place centre back and centre front of blocks 2 to $2\frac{1}{2}$ inches (according to desired fullness) away from perpendicular edges of paper. Lengthen and raise shoulders $\frac{1}{2}$ inch. Increase bust $\frac{1}{2}$ inch. Lower armhole 1 inch. Lower front neck line 1 inch or desired depth. Re-shape pattern lines. Measure down from top of shoulder on both back and front the depth of yoke required (6 inches to 8 inches), then rule off this depth.

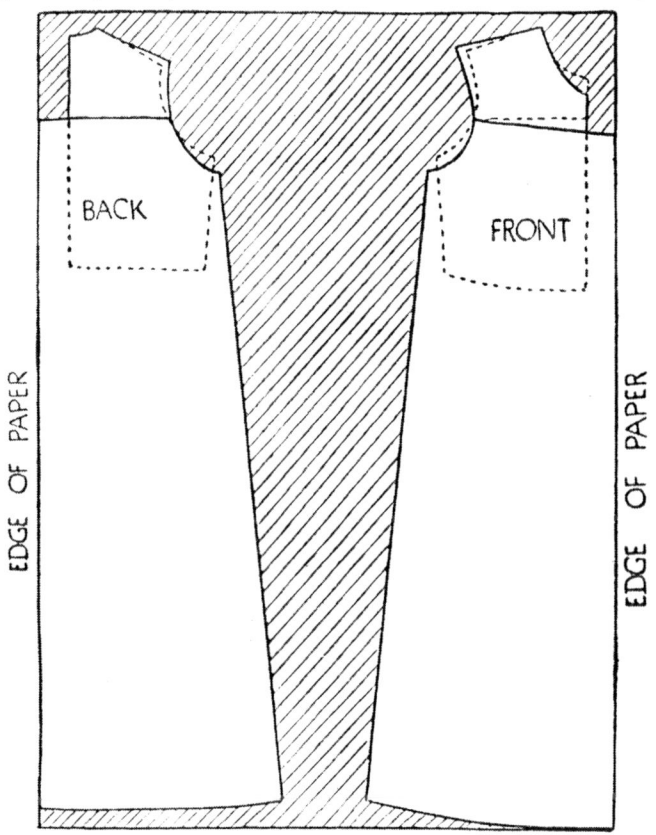

FIG. 92

Measure down 1 inch from yoke line at centre front and curve to meet yoke at armhole. Cut out the yoke as outlined, and the top of the skirt line to the edges of paper back and front (the amount of fullness allowed on back and front).

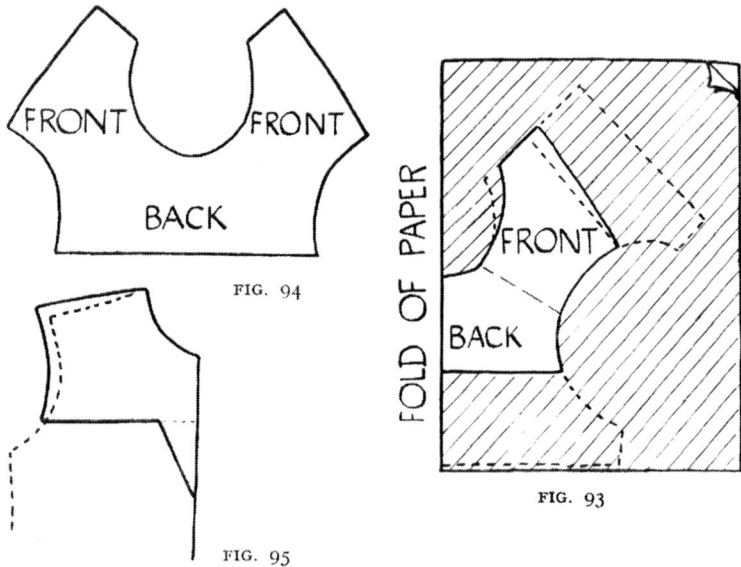

FIG. 94

FIG. 95

FIG. 93

To cut a Saddle Yoke (Fig. 93). An alternative method for Yoke A.

When a yoke is cut all in one without a seam on the shoulders it is known as a saddle yoke. It is well to remember that for this shape the pattern must fit perfectly at the shoulder as no alteration is possible when it is once cut out in material. It is advisable to obtain the whole of the yoke pattern as it can then more easily be fitted to the figure and tested. For the pattern take paper, fold it, and place the back and front sections of the block together as shown (Fig. 93), the two shoulder lines meeting and the centre back to the fold of paper. Outline the upper part of the combined patterns. Rule off the depth of yoke required at back and front and lower front neck line 1 inch. Fig. 94 shows the completed yoke opened out.

BODICE TYPE PATTERNS

The method of cutting Yoke B is clearly indicated in Fig. 95.

To cut Yoke C (Fig. 96)

This style of yoke is usually expressed in lace though it looks equally attractive if the material of the yoke is tucked either horizontally or perpendicularly.

Fig. 96 shows how to produce Yoke C.

To cut Yoke D (Fig. 97)

Outline blocks on to paper and adapt shoulder and bust lines. Dot a line across back and front, 2 inches more or less above the waist line. Raise the adapted back waist line ¾ inch, and lower the adapted front waist line 1 to 1½ inches. This will keep the bodice level all round when on the wearer, and prevent the skirt falling in ugly lines.

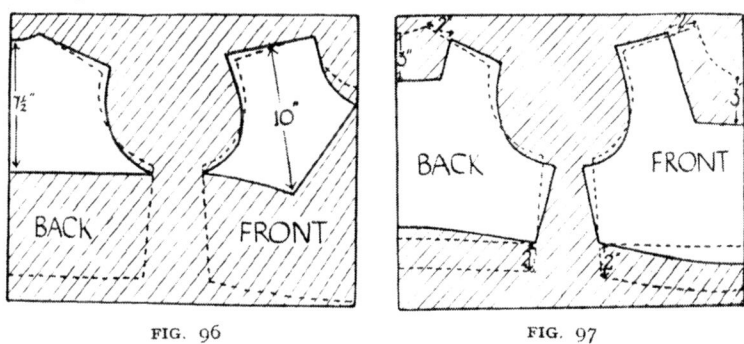

FIG. 96   FIG. 97

SMOCK OVERALL (Fig. 98)

Sometimes the pattern of one part of a garment can be used for cutting the corresponding part of another. The pattern of nightgown A may be adapted for the smock overall (Fig. 98).

Cut yoke as described for nightgown and make overall about 36 inches long. Extend the width of pattern below front yoke for twice the width of smocking. Adapt the back pattern in a similar manner allowing less fullness at the back than at the front. Either of the collars (Fig. 87 or Fig. 88) may be used. The yoke patterns may also be adapted for blouses and jumpers. Refer to style yoke (Fig. 71).

DRESSING-GOWNS AND COAT OVERALLS (cut from bodice block)

The similarity of garments will be noted as one progresses in pattern making, and it will be found that one pattern will cut quite a number of garments similar in construction. Dressing-gowns and coat overalls differ principally in length so the pattern of Fig. 99 may be used for the overall and dressing-gown (Fig. 100), and also for dressing-gown (Fig. 101). Up-to-date style features can be introduced into the overalls by varying the neck line and the trimming. Figs. 100 and 101 illustrate two popular and practical styles of dressing-gowns with snug-fitting roll over collars. These collars are also suitable for the coat overalls.

THE PATTERN, FIG. 99

Place centre back of block to a perpendicular edge of paper, and centre front of block 5 inches away from opposite edge, and outline.

Lengthen shoulders $\frac{1}{2}$ inch. Lower armhole 1 inch. Widen bust $\frac{1}{2}$ inch on back and front blocks.

Back

AC = desired length of gown from shoulder to ankle.

BC = additional length from waist to hem line.

FIG. 98

BODICE TYPE PATTERNS

CD = ¼ desired hem width minus 1 inch.

Front

BC = additional length from front waist line—BC of back.

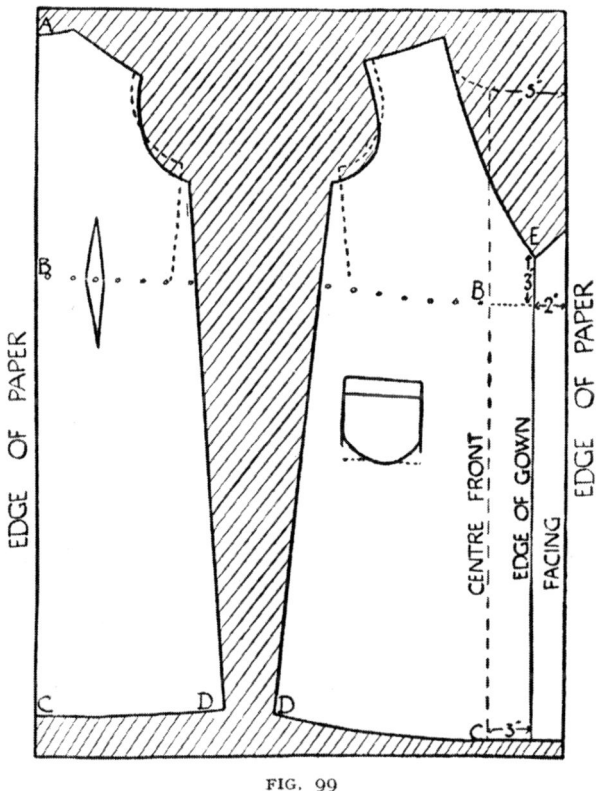

FIG. 99

CD = ¼ desired hem width plus 1 inch. Add on at centre front line a wrap of 3 inches, and a facing of 2 inches.

E = a movable point (3 inches above waist line according to style of neck line required.

FIG. 100

BODICE TYPE PATTERNS

Note shaping of facing at E. Unless cut as shown the edge of the facing will fail to meet the neck line and difficulty will be experienced in attaching the collar, or finishing the neck line.

The method of obtaining the collar patterns is described on page 77.

DRESSING JACKETS

Can be cut from the dressing-gown pattern (Fig. 99), by using only the top part, and omitting the skirt. The jackets vary according to taste, but an average length is 26 inches, from shoulder to hem. Draw a line across the back and front pattern at the requisite length, and cut it off along this line or fold up the surplus length as described on page 9.

MAGYAR PATTERN WITH SHOULDER SEAM

The Magyar pattern (Fig. 102) is another adaptation of the bodice type pattern. The centre back and front of Magyar pattern is indicated by a dotted line from neck point of bodice block, to E on the hem line. It will be observed that the shoulder and underarm lines of the bodice block are extended to form the sleeve section.

FIG. 101

90 GERTRUDE MASON'S PATTERN BOOK

The Magyar adapted from the block together with the introduction of a shoulder seam is a great help in obtaining a satisfactory fit around the arms when the body section of

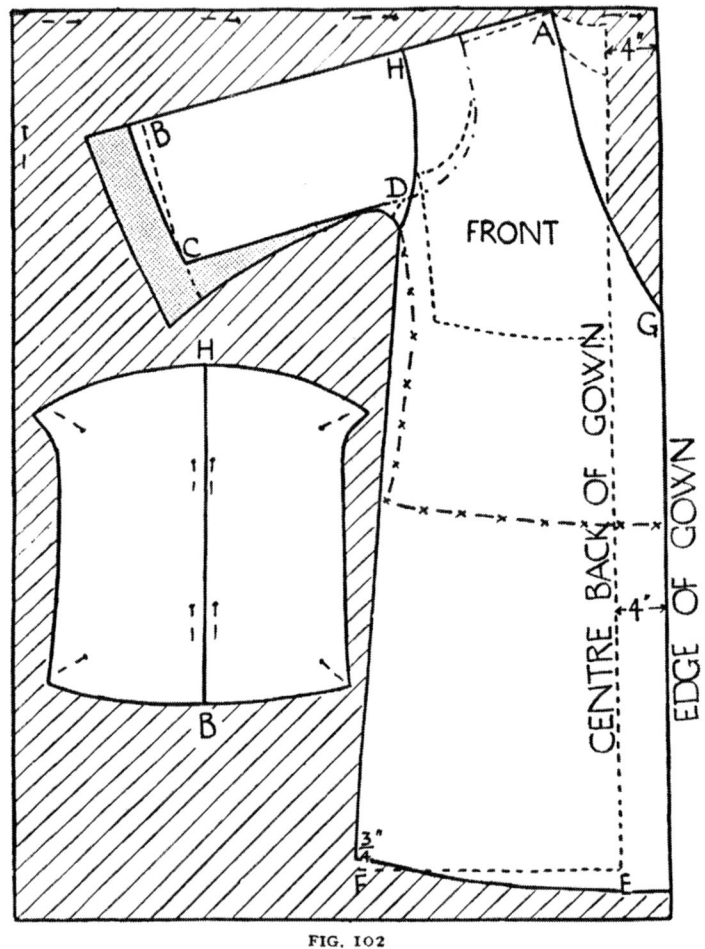

FIG. 102

this type of garment is required to be close fitting. The original Magyar illustrated and dealt with in Chapter 4 is cut in one piece and has no shoulder seam.

BODICE TYPE PATTERNS 91

EMBROIDERED KIMONO (Fig. 103)

THE PATTERN, FIG. 102

Take two large sheets of paper and pin them together. The upper sheet is for the front of the Magyar pattern with

FIG. 103

wrap over, and the under sheet is for the back section. Place centre front line of block 4 inches (or more if wider wrap is required) away from perpendicular edges of paper, and with shoulder line A touching the top edges (Fig. 102). Outline and remove block. Raise shoulder ½ inch, widen bust 1 inch, lower armhole 1 inch; re-shape pattern lines and mark point D. Extend shoulder line from A to B the desired length of sleeve (19 to 23 inches).

C = width of sleeve squared down from B (6½ to 7½ inches). Add ½ inch of round and curve to C. Rule seam of sleeve CD.

Note.—Shaded part of sleeve indicates how the sleeve may be made longer and wider for the embroidered kimono (Fig. 103). Extend centre back line to desired length of gown.

EF = ¼ desired width of gown. Rule from DF and raise

FIG. 104

BODICE TYPE PATTERNS 93

F ¾ inch. Measure 1 inch diagonally from D and re-shape underarm line as shown in diagram (Fig. 102). G is a movable point. Lower front edge 1 inch and complete front pattern. To complete back section cut off the extension

FIG. 105

94 GERTRUDE MASON'S PATTERN BOOK

of paper allowed for front wrap, and adapt back neck line as desired. The square kimono sleeve cut all in one with the garment as shown (Fig. 102), can only be cut if the material is wide enough. When a join is necessary, simulate a set in sleeve, and cut an armhole in the pattern as shown HD. H is a movable point 2 to 4 inches beyond the shoulder of the bodice block. To cut the sleeve section without a seam pin the two pieces of the sleeve together on to paper and cut out whole (Fig. 102).

The slip-on coat illustrated (Fig. 104) is similar in construction to the kimono, differing principally in the style of front. To

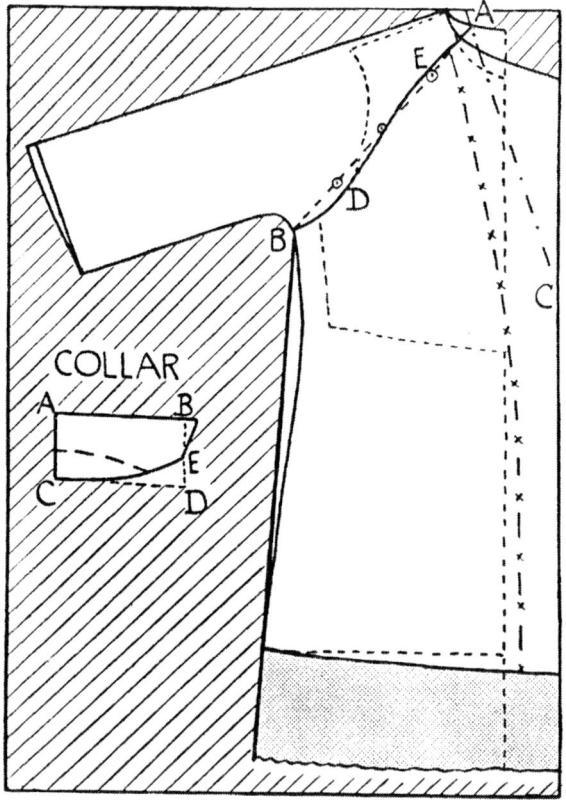

FIG. 106

BODICE TYPE PATTERNS

adapt the pattern, rule from A to E for the front edge of the coat and pleat up the surplus width at the lower edge of the sleeve. This type of coat can be made of heavy or light material to match or contrast with the dress or skirt. A large amount of variety can be obtained by altering the neck line and the finishing.

A dressing jacket or short sac coat can be cut from the pattern (Fig. 102) by using only the top part. The length of the jacket varies according to personal requirements. A useful length is 26 inches from shoulder to hem, and this is indicated on Fig. 102 by a dot and cross line.

The Magyar pattern may also be used as a basis draft from which all varieties of this class of garment can be produced.

DRESSING-GOWN WITH RAGLAN SLEEVE (Fig. 105). (Cut from Magyar pattern)

THE PATTERN, FIG. 106

Outline on double paper the Magyar pattern of Fig. 102. Raise centre front neck line 1 inch and shape lapels. C is a movable point and denotes the bottom of the lapel crease line (see dot and dash line).

For Raglan Sleeve

Measure $1\frac{1}{2}$ to 2 inches from front shoulder point along neck line and mark A. Rule line AB and divide it into quarters. Hollow $\frac{1}{2}$ inch at D, and add $\frac{1}{4}$ inch of round at E.

The Facing

Cut a facing pattern the exact shape of the front of the gown measuring 1 inch wide at the top and 2 to $2\frac{1}{2}$ inches at lower hem (dash and cross lines).

The Collar

AB = half the neck measure of garment from centre back to within 2 inches of end of lapel.

AC = depth of collar (3 inches). Rule in the rectangle.

BE = the collar end — $\frac{1}{4}$ inch less than the closed edge of lapel ($1\frac{3}{4}$ inches) and $\frac{1}{2}$ inch to the right.

Complete collar as shown (Fig. 106).

The Raglan sleeve pattern (Fig. 106) may be used for a swagger coat.

VI

A SHAPED ONE-PIECE FOUNDATION PATTERN

It will be observed that up to the present all the adapted garments have been loose-fitting, with more or less straight underarm seams, and with the surplus width or fullness disposed of in tucks, or drawn in by a ribbon or sash. We now come to more advanced fashion garments, cut on slim lines. In order to obtain the smart cut and sleek fitting that these modern garments demand, it is advisable to use a shapely one-piece foundation. This is produced by combining the straight top petticoat pattern, with the bodice pattern as depicted (Fig. 107).

Method. Take the back and front sections of the straight top petticoat pattern and pin the bust line of each to the back and front bust line of bodice block. Outline the combined blocks in this position on to firm paper, trace through waist and hip lines, and then cut out. This foundation pattern may be adapted to any style of garment for both day and night wear.

ADAPTATIONS OF SHAPED ONE-PIECE FOUNDATION PATTERN

Princess Petticoats with round and square neck lines
THE PATTERN, FIG. 108

Place centre front of one-piece foundation to a fold of paper and outline. Mark in back neck line using back of foundation pattern. Test length of pattern from shoulder to hem line and increase or decrease according to length of petticoat required.

A SHAPED ONE-PIECE FOUNDATION

For Round Neck

A. Lower front neck line 3½ inches or desired depth.
B. Lower back neck line 3 inches or desired depth.
Find centre of shoulder line and mark a dot.
CD = 2 inches, or desired width of shoulder measured equally each side of the dot. Shape as shown (Fig. 108).

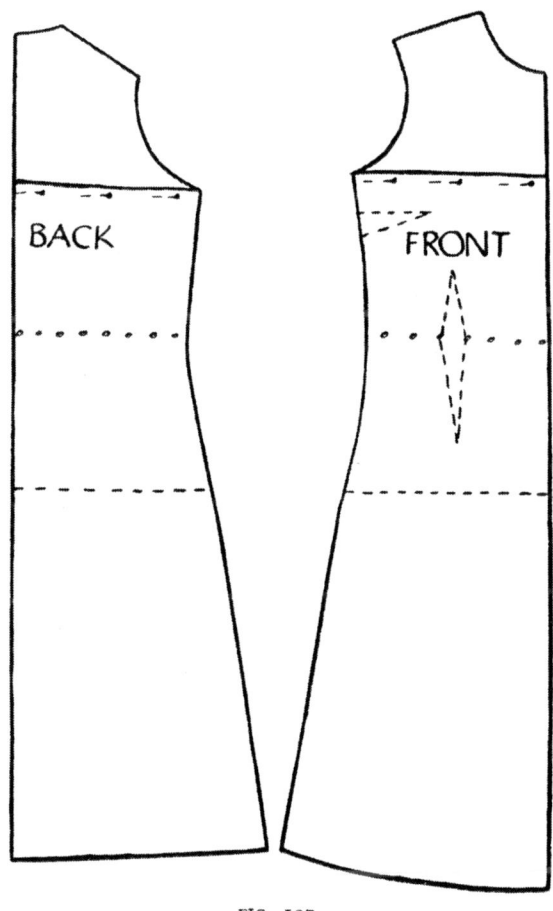

FIG. 107

For Square Neck

Dot and dash lines of Fig. 108 indicate adaptation. Make shoulder width CD 1 inch.

PYJAMAS. Cut from foundation pattern.

Fig. 109 A and C shows pyjamas of practical design, smart but sensible. The bound scalloped front of A is very effective and the sleeves and collar carry out the same style feature.

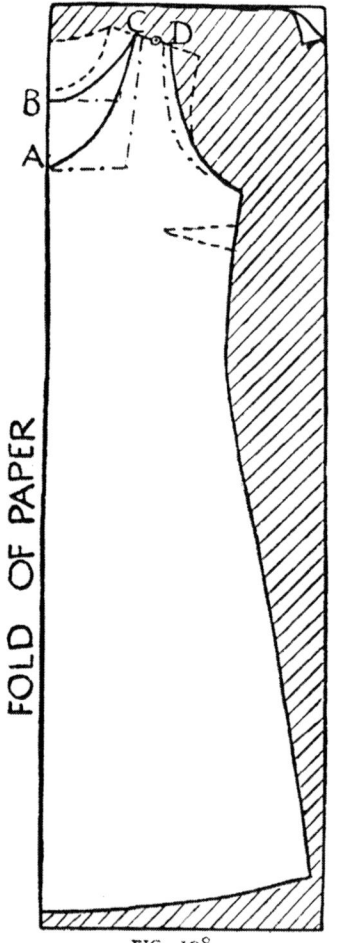

FIG. 108

There is a peasant air about the cosy pyjamas of Style C, and the effect is accentuated by the embroidery.

THE PATTERNS OF A AND C

Outline back and front of foundation pattern 4 to 7 inches below waist line. Raise ends of shoulder ½ inch. Lower armhole ½ inch. Widen bust 1 inch. For Style A, cut neck line as drafted. For Style B add on 1½ inches to centre front line for front fastening. Use sleeve pattern (Fig. 75), and trouser pattern (Fig. 132).

PYJAMAS (Fig. 109B)

For lounging or sleeping, with matching coatee, which lend themselves to silk or cotton material trimmed with bias binding.

THE PYJAMA BLOUSE (Fig. 109B)

THE PATTERN, FIG. 110

Outline back and front of foundation pattern 3 inches

A SHAPED ONE-PIECE FOUNDATION

below waist line (for blousing and casing for elastic). Raise ends of shoulder ½ inch. Lower armhole ½ inch. Widen bust 1 inch.

Back

    A is midway shoulder line.

    B = 3 inches. If a lower neck line is desired rule from A as indicated by dot and dash line.

FIG. 109

Front

A is midway shoulder.

B = 2 inches from centre front neck point.

C = depth of desired yoke 5 to 5½ inches.

Trace off yoke section which is shown (Fig. 110).

The front edge of the yoke must be lowered about 1 inch (see dotted line) to arrange for a little fullness. This is pleated up as suggested (Fig. 109B), under a large bow.

CROSSOVER COATEE with flared basque and sleeves (Fig. 109B)

THE PATTERN, FIG. 111

Back

Place centre back of foundation pattern to edge of paper and outline upper part 4 to 5 inches below waist line. Widen bust ½ inch. Lower armhole 1 inch; re-shape armhole and underarm lines (Fig. 111).

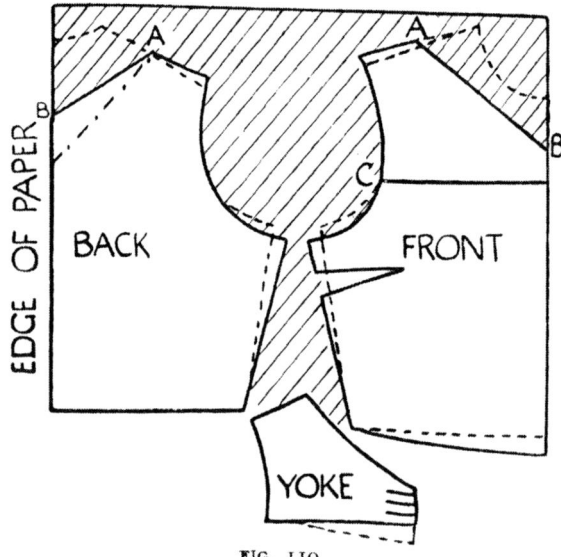

FIG. 110

A SHAPED ONE-PIECE FOUNDATION

Front

Place centre front of foundation pattern 7 inches inside opposite edge of paper and outline upper part 4 to 5 inches below waist line. Note that the coatee has a shoulder dart and, therefore, the underarm dart is not required. For shoulder dart measure 1 inch (or more) horizontally from shoulder point. Widen bust ½ inch. Lower armhole 1 inch. Re-draw shoulder, armhole, and underarm lines (Fig. 111). Shape for crossover front from neck point to lower edge as shown (Fig. 111).

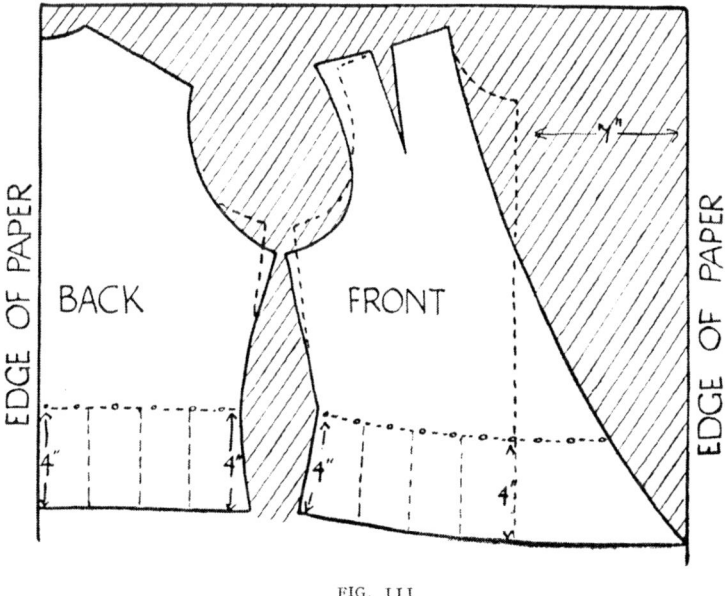

FIG. 111

For Flared Basque

Cut off the back and front basque sections (dot and dash lines) and cut up pattern pieces where indicated by dotted lines. Separate cut edges amount of flare required (½ inch to 1 inch) (Fig. 112), pin in position on to paper, pencil round the new outlines and cut out.

The pattern of the flared sleeve is shown (Fig. 78, page 72). Use the trouser pattern described on page 120.

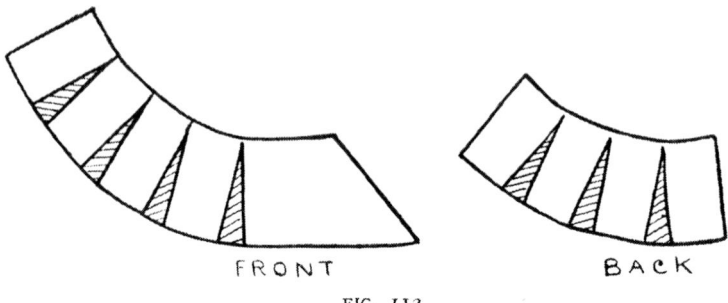

FIG. 112

The pattern of the crossover coatee (Fig. 111) can be used with slight modifications for other garments similar in construction, only more elaborate as illustrated (Fig. 113). The quality of the cloth and the fur banding adds a luxurious effect. For the skirt, see page 131.

A BOLERO (Fig. 114)

Boleros are very adaptable and may be worn over a dress, or in conjunction with a sun-suit, or pyjamas similar in style to Fig. 109B.

THE PATTERN

Outline foundation pattern to the waist line. Measure out 1 inch from centre back and rule new centre back line. Mark the required amount above the waist line $1\frac{1}{2}$ to 2 inches. Extend front shoulder line 1 inch for a small dart. Re-shape armhole, and draw new shoulder line. Mark required amount above waist line. Rule a new centre front line from shoulder to lower edge. The amount cut away in front depends on style and personal preference, usually $1\frac{1}{2}$ to $2\frac{1}{2}$ inches. The corners may be square, or round as Fig. 114.

A SHAPED ONE-PIECE FOUNDATION

FIG. 113

NIGHTDRESS WITH BLOUSE TOP complete with bishop sleeve and Eton collar, allied with a long straight skirt (Fig. 115).

This is a very plain but smart nightgown for the woman who prefers her night attire to have a tailored air.

THE PATTERN, FIG. 116

Place centre back of foundation pattern to a perpendicular edge of paper, and centre front 2 inches away from opposite edge of paper. Extend back and front sections to desired length of nightgown. Raise and lengthen shoulder lines ½ inch. Widen bust ½ inch. Lower armholes ½ inch.

Back

AB	—	additional length required.
BC	—	¼ total width of garment, or 15½ to 17½ inches according to weight of material. Re-shape underarm line, and make CD = AB.
E	—	4 inches (more or less) above waist line.

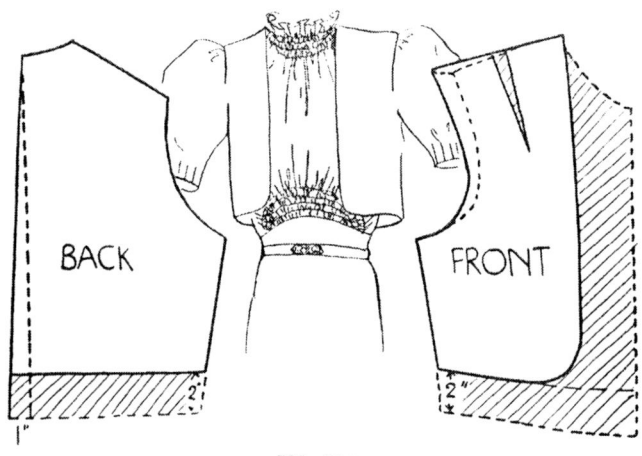

FIG. 114

A SHAPED ONE-PIECE FOUNDATION

Front

AB = additional length required equals AB of back pattern.
BC = $\frac{1}{4}$ total width of garment (see back).
CD = CD of back.
E = $4\frac{1}{2}$ inches above front waist line.
F = 2 inches, the allowance for tucks or darts on blouse line. Re-shape underarm line and curve to E. Add on $1\frac{1}{2}$ inches beyond centre front line for fastening. Note shape at neck line. Cut out back and front blouse sections along style lines FE. For sleeve pattern see Fig. 75A.

SLEEVELESS NIGHTDRESS with tucks on shoulder and graduated tucks at front style line (Fig. 117)

THE PATTERN, FIG. 118

Place back of block to a perpendicular edge of paper and front block 2 inches in from opposite edge of paper. Outline and mark in waist line. Raise and lengthen shoulder points $\frac{1}{2}$ inch. Widen bust $\frac{1}{2}$ inch. Lower armhole $\frac{1}{2}$ inch. Widen neck 2 inches on back and front shoulder (Fig. 118). Lower back neck 2 inches.

Front

Lower front neck line 6 inches and shape as shown (Fig. 118).

FIG. 115

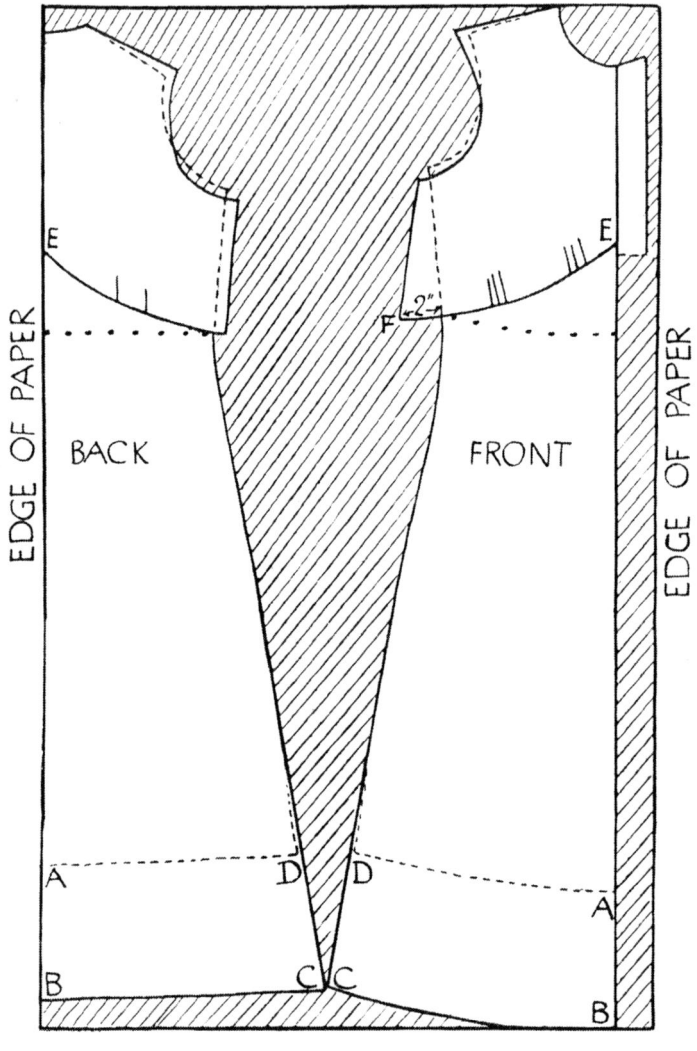

FIG. 116

For tucks on shoulder

Extend shoulder and bust lines 1½ inches; re-shape armhole. Draw in side seam extending ½ inch at waist line, then shape style line as shown (Fig. 118).

For tucks at centre front

Extend 1½ inches beyond centre front line of skirt section. Note shape of extension.

SQUARE NECK NIGHTDRESS with gauged side pieces, and front and back panel (Fig. 119A)

THE PATTERN, FIG. 120

Outline foundation pattern on to paper as previously described. Lower armhole ½ inch. Widen bust ½ inch.

Back

A = 4 inches. Measure out from A 3 inches.
      Rule a perpendicular line to B, a point 1½ inches below the waist line.
C = Middle of shoulder line.
D = 1 inch above waist line.
      Complete back as shown (Fig. 120).

Front

A = 5 inches down from neck point.
      Measure from A width of panel (3 inches).
      Complete the front.

Trace off on to paper the back and front side pieces which are CB and D of draft, shown (Fig. 122). Note that the back and front panels are a continuation of the skirt section (Fig. 120). The front panel is shown (Fig. 121).

To lessen the severity of the style, and to give a graceful line over the bust, the edge of the front side piece is gauged.

FIG. 117

To allow fullness for the gauging

Cut up the front side piece as indicated by dotted lines (Fig. 122). Separate the cut edges 1 to 1½ inches and pin on to paper (Fig. 123). Outline in this position and then cut out. This style is very becoming for day or evening gowns. Gauging may be introduced at the centre front of a garment in exactly the same way. Note gauging on dress (Fig. 114).

A SHAPED ONE-PIECE FOUNDATION

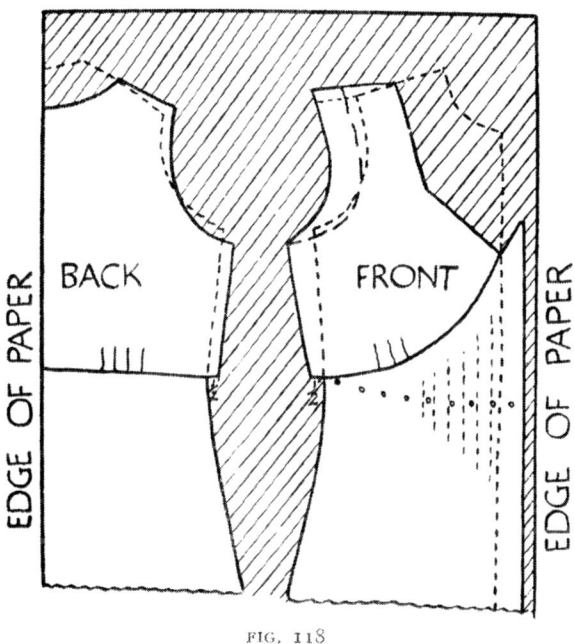

FIG. 118

STYLE NIGHTDRESS with cowl or draped neck line (Fig. 119B)

The cowl neck line is a modern type of neck drapery. It is formed from a triangle of material built on to the front pattern of the garment. When cut out in material this triangle sags considerably between the two points of support, *i.e.*, the shoulders, and forms curves or drapery.

The cowl neck line inset in the nightdress with faggot stitching has a new appeal when combined in the style of Fig. 119B.

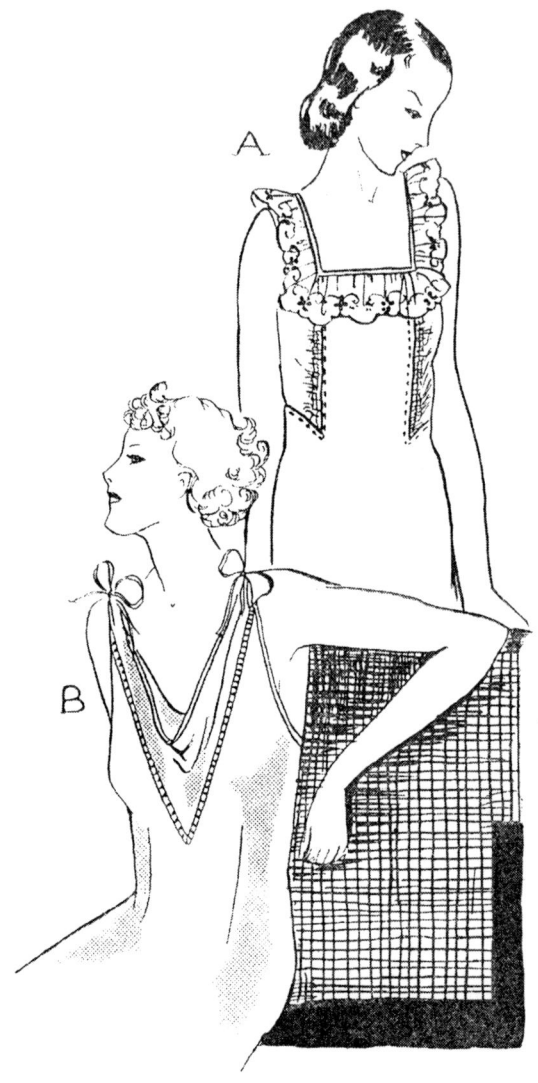

FIG. 119

A SHAPED ONE-PIECE FOUNDATION

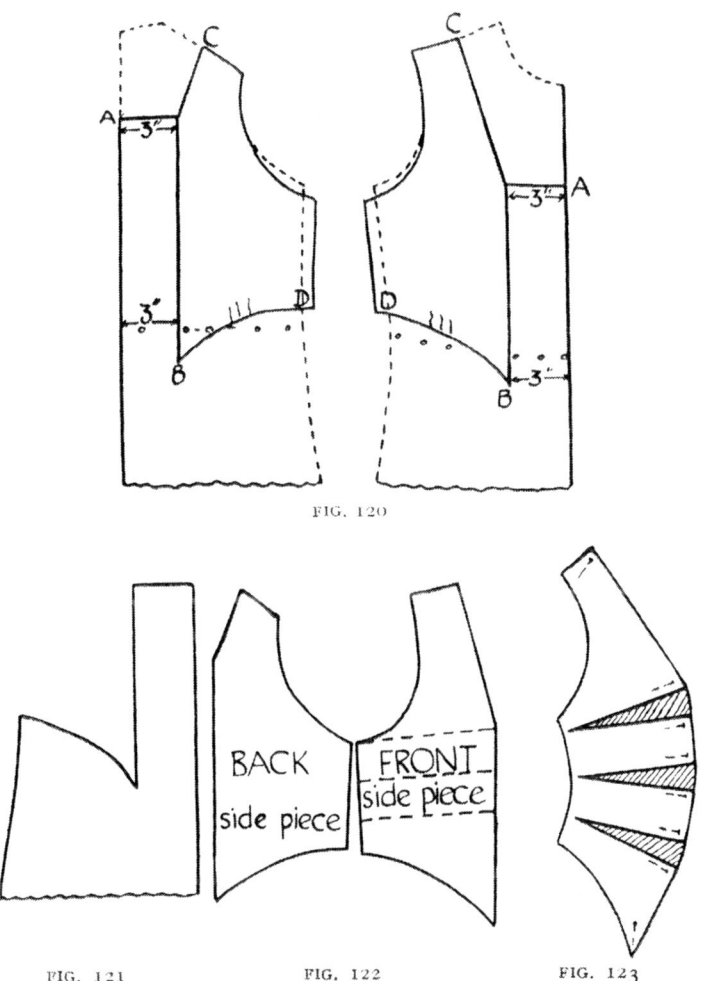

FIG. 120

FIG. 121   FIG. 122   FIG. 123

THE PATTERN, FIG. 124

Place back line of block to perpendicular edge of paper, and front line of block 6 inches inside opposite edge of paper. Find centre of back and front shoulders and mark a dot (Fig. 124).

Back

A   =   5 inches, or desired depth of back neck.
BC =   1 inch (more or less) rule BC and BA.
D   =   Armhole lowered 2½ inches. Shape style armhole CD.

Front

A   =   3 inches above waist line.
BC =   1 inch.
D   =   2½ inches.
E   =   1½ inches above centre front neck line. Mark a dot on the centre front line at level of bust line (see diagram) (Fig. 124). Measure the distance from C to the dot (indicated by dotted lines) and measure out this amount from C to F. Rule from C to F passing through E, and then rule F to A. When cutting in material FA is placed to a crossway fold.

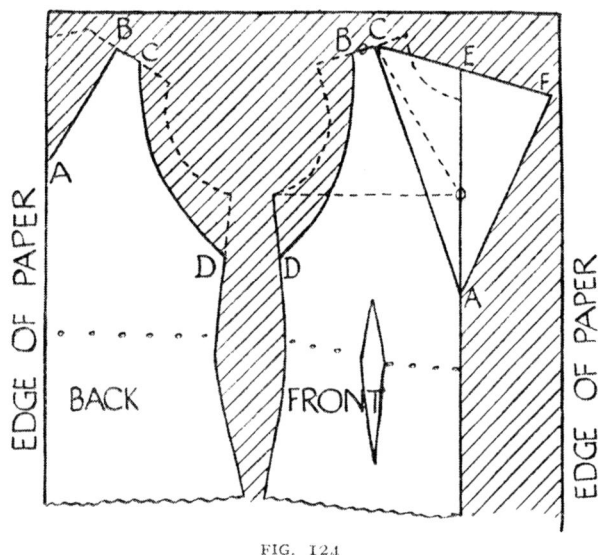

FIG. 124

A SHAPED ONE-PIECE FOUNDATION

Fig. 125 shows two versions of the cowl or draped neck line suitable for frock or jumpers.

1. Held in 3 pleats with ornamental clip.
2. Cut in with style front of garment (see diagram).

It will be found that an extension of 4 inches beyond the centre front line (Fig. 125) will produce satisfactory folds. If drapery is required to be quite slack and the folds triangular as illustrated in the second version (Fig. 125), then this amount must be increased accordingly. Some cowls are arranged on the back neck of a garment and may be worn over the head.

A detachable cowl may be formed from a triangle of georgette, silk, or similar draping material. Cut a 20-inch or a 30-inch (according to amount of drapery required) square of paper diagonally. At centre of diagonal measure down 1½ inches and slope to corners. Pin to corner of material and cut out. Have all edges of triangle picoted. Lightly attach to centre back, centre front, or shoulder of garment, and knot ends of triangle together. It is essential to the effect of any garment where drapery is introduced that the folds shall be graceful and definite, and not untidy.

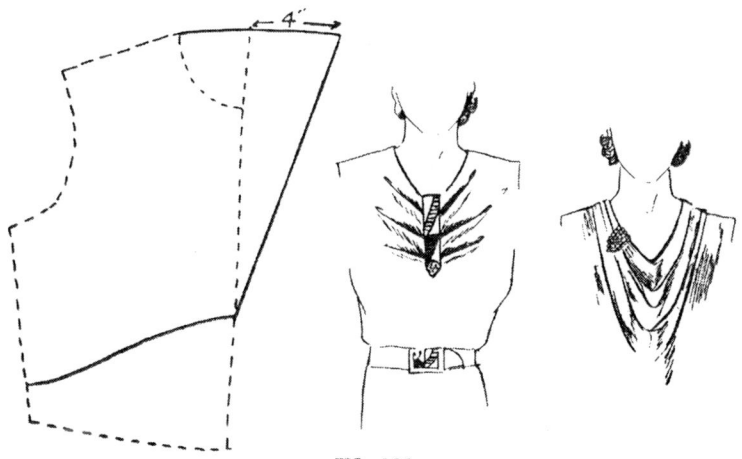

FIG. 125

VII

KNICKER TYPE PATTERN

KNICKERS is the name given to the undergarments extending from the waist and covering the lower limbs to about the knee.

KNICKERS FOR DAY AND EVENING WEAR

Skilfully cut, well-fitting knickers, without any unnecessary fullness are essential for the slim-fitting dresses of to-day. Ill-fitting knickers are the most uncomfortable and the most exasperating of garments. Knickers should fit closely and unobtrusively and should have sufficient back body length to allow for freedom of movement. A simple reliable draft of knickers drawn to individual measures is given (Fig. 126). This pattern lends itself to making up in several ways. It can be used for the severely simple knickers with elastic at waist and knee (Fig. 127) or adapted to very slimming lines with front yoke and wide legs (Fig. 129). Fig. 126 is also the standard block from which a variety of knickers and pyjama trousers can be developed.

THE KNICKER PATTERN, FIG. 126
Measurements required:
    1. Waist: Taken easily (Figs. 1 and 2).
    2. Hips: Taken loosely round the fullest part of the figure (Figs. 1 and 2).
    3. Side length: Taken from the waist to the knee when kneeling (Fig. 3).

Size of paper required:
    1. Length: Side length plus 6 inches.
    3. Width: The hip measure.

KNICKER TYPE PATTERN

Fold paper in half in the width and keep fold to left-hand side. Measure 4 inches below edge of paper on fold for the hip slope and mark A (Fig. 126).

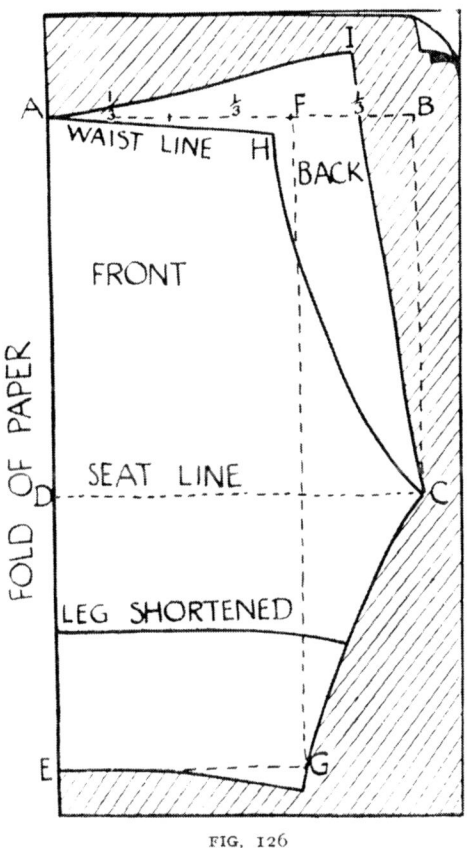

FIG. 126

AB = ⅜ of the whole hip measure.
BC = the same measurement as AB.
CD = AB. Draw dotted lines as shown in diagram.
AE = side length measure. Divide AB into thirds and rule dotted line FG. H is ¾ inch down and ¾ inch (or more) to the left of F.

Shape for the front body line from H to C as shown in diagram. Draw the front waist line from H to A. I is half FB and raised same amount. Draw back body line IC.

FIG. 127

Note.—I can be moved near to F if less fullness is required at waist line. The waist line should measure half hip measure plus 1 to 1½ inches to allow for easy slipping on and off.

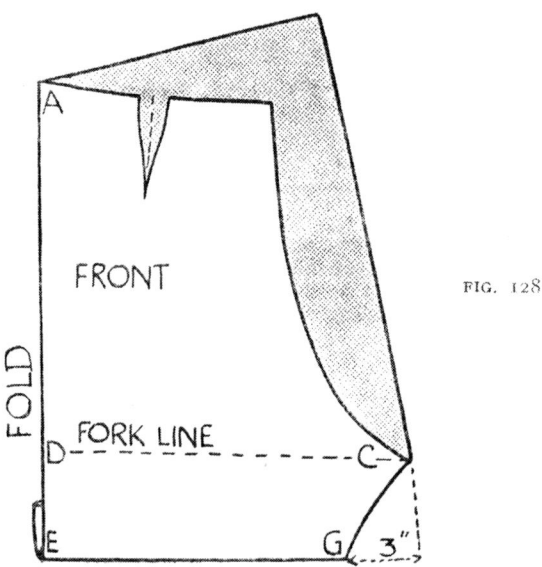

FIG. 128

KNICKER TYPE PATTERN

Curve for back waist line AI. Cut through the double paper on back body lines, then open out paper and cut front body line and waist line. Shorten knickers to individual requirements. For elastic at knees drop G ¾ inch (Fig. 126), this prevents the leg seam dragging.

KNICKERS WITH FRENCH LEGS

Fold under lower edge of knicker pattern to length required. For wider or French legs measure out from G 2½ to 3½ inches and shape as indicated by dotted lines (Fig. 128). Fullness at front waist may be darted as shown.

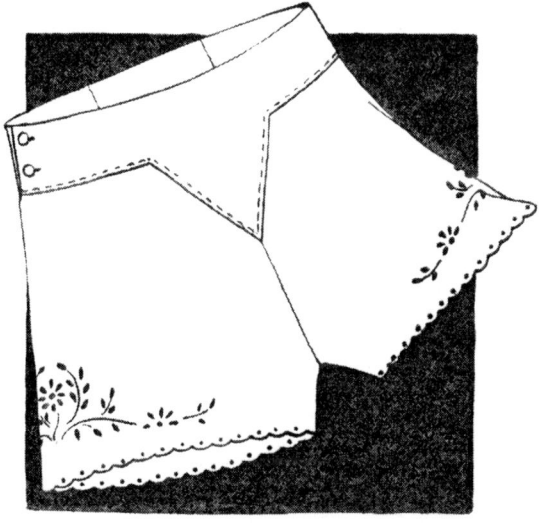

FIG. 129

YOKED KNICKERS with side fastening (cut from knicker pattern) (Fig. 129)

THE YOKE PATTERN, FIG. 130

Outline knicker pattern on to paper and shape front yoke section as clearly illustrated (Fig. 130). Suppress surplus fullness at back waist as follows :— Divide back waist width

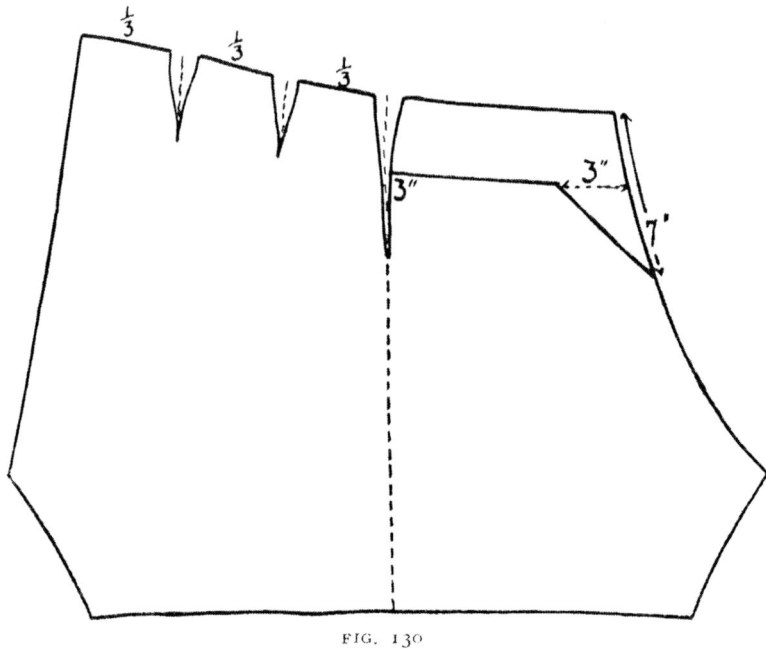

FIG. 130

into thirds, square a line at each third about 3½ inches long for length of dart. Take out ½ inch to ¾ inch each side this dotted line as shown (Fig. 130). Do not cut the darts until after fitting. Arrange an opening in the side seam as shown.

PYJAMA TROUSERS (Fig. 131). (Cut from knicker pattern)

Fig. 132 illustrates the cutting of modern close-fitting trousers with side openings suitable for lounging or sleeping.

Measurements required:

Side length (Fig. 2).

Width of seat. Taken 10 inches below waist line.

Take knicker pattern (Fig. 126) and measure from C along the fork line ⅓ the whole seat measure. Fold back the surplus width from A to D (striped section in diagram) (Fig. 132).

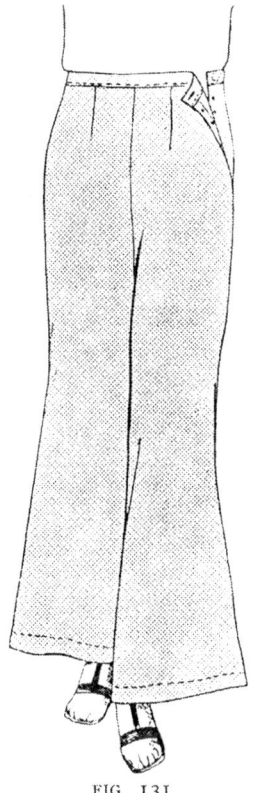

FIG. 131

Place this creased edge to a fold of paper, pin in position, and outline knicker pattern to fork line only. Remove pattern, fill in the waist line and mark A^2 as shown (Fig. 132).

$A^2 E =$ side length measure.

$EG =$ 9 inches or half desired width of trouser legs.

Rule a dotted line CG, and divide it into thirds. Mark 1 inch to the left of the first third below C. Shape leg seam from C passing through this point to G. Extra width may be added to the legs as indicated by dot and dash lines. To reduce the width of the waist line make a pleat, or take out a dart midway back and front waist line as shown (Fig. 132). If side seams are required cut up the fold AE.

PYJAMA TROUSERS without side fastening.

For trousers of thin material or of the style illustrated (Fig. 109), darts and openings are not necessary. The extra fullness is drawn in with elastic, or pyjama cord.

When no opening is desired use the knicker pattern (Fig. 126) and place AD to the fold, and follow instructions for Fig. 132. Make waist line half hip measure plus 1 inch.

CIRCULAR KNICKERS (cut from knicker pattern)

This type of knicker is sleek-fitting at waist and hip line, flaring out into wide legs—a most becoming style for evening wear. They are cut so as to dispense with a yoke or elastic at waist thus eliminating unsightly ridges under a form-fitting gown. The waist edge is neatened with a crossway false hem.

THE PATTERN, FIG. 133

Outline knicker pattern (Fig. 126) on to paper. Cut down the side line and then cut back and front in half, and number the pieces as shown (Fig. 134). Pin the four pieces of pattern on to paper, overlap waist and hip lines (shaded dotted portion) but widen out 3 to 4 inches between each piece at lower edge (Fig. 135). Test the waist and hip measurements.

The waist line should measure half waist plus 1 to 1½ inches.

The hip line should measure half hips plus 1 to 1½ inches.

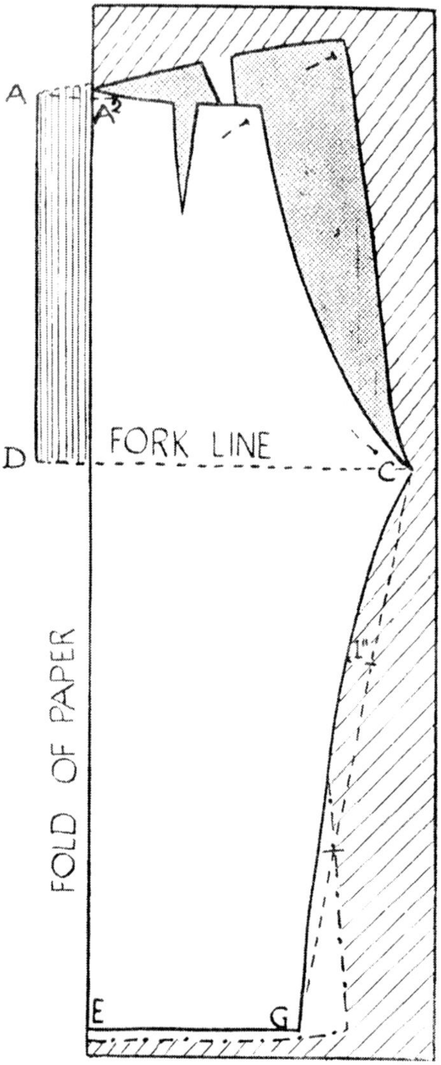

FIG. 132

When correct, pencil in the new outline, and cut out. The circular knicker pattern is shown (Fig. 133).

KNICKER TYPE PATTERN

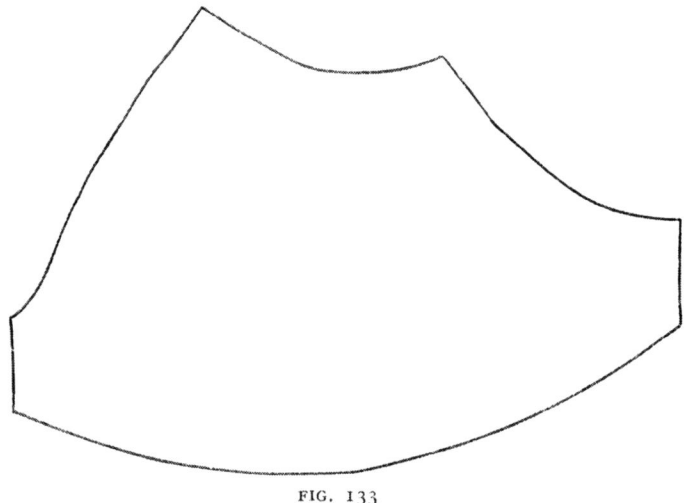

FIG. 133

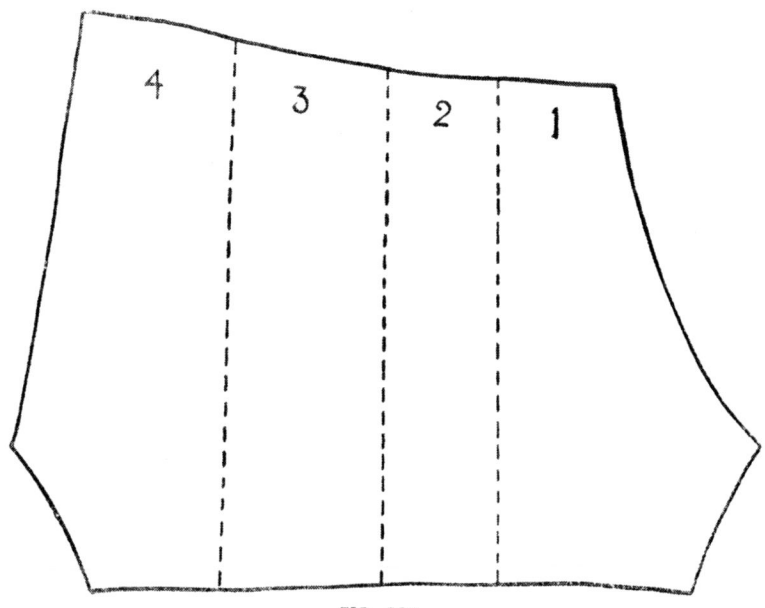

FIG. 134

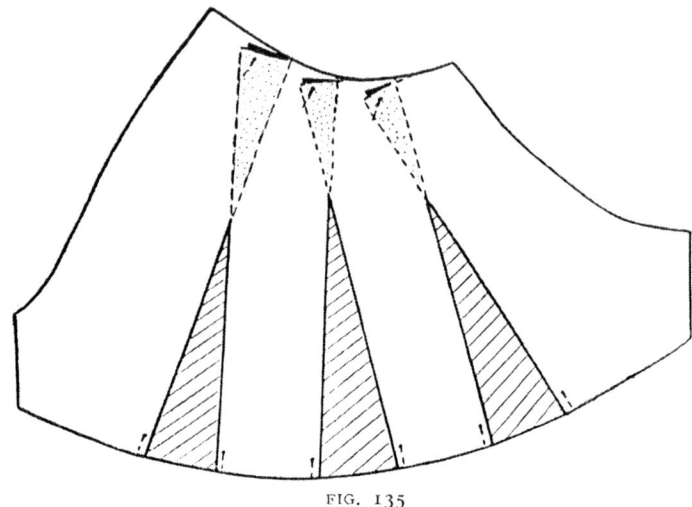

FIG. 135

SKIRT KNICKERS

When dresses fit closely to the hips it is essential that the undergarments shall fit closely also. This new style of knickers is cut on the lines of a two-piece skirt plus a fork at front and back. They fit the figure very closely and flatly at the waist and hips but become very full just below the seat.

DRAFT OF SKIRT KNICKERS, FIG. 136

Measurements required:

1. Waist (Figs. 1 and 2).
2. Hips (Figs. 1 and 2).
3. Seat depth (Fig. 4).
4. Length of leg seam (personal requirements).

The knickers of Fig. 136 have been drafted to the following measurements :—

1. Waist .. .. 28 inches
2. Hips .. .. 39 ,,
3. Seat depth .. .. 12 ,,
4. Leg seam .. .. $3\frac{1}{2}$,,

KNICKER TYPE PATTERN

Draw two lines at right angles.

A is at the right-hand corner.

AB	=	half hip measure minus 3 inches.
AC	=	3 inches. Rule BC.
CD	=	8 inches.
DE	=	half hip measure plus ½ inch.
CF	=	seat depth plus 1 inch.
FG	=	length of leg seam required, 3 to 5 inches.

Rule from B through E and on to H.
Make centre back line 1 inch longer than centre front line CG. Connect H and G.

HI = GF.

J is midway BC and 1 inch down.

Curve for waist line from B through J and on to C.
Rule a line from J through midway ED and HG.
Make the side line JK ½ inch longer than CG the front line. Suppress 1 inch on side line and shape as shown (Fig. 136). It will be noticed

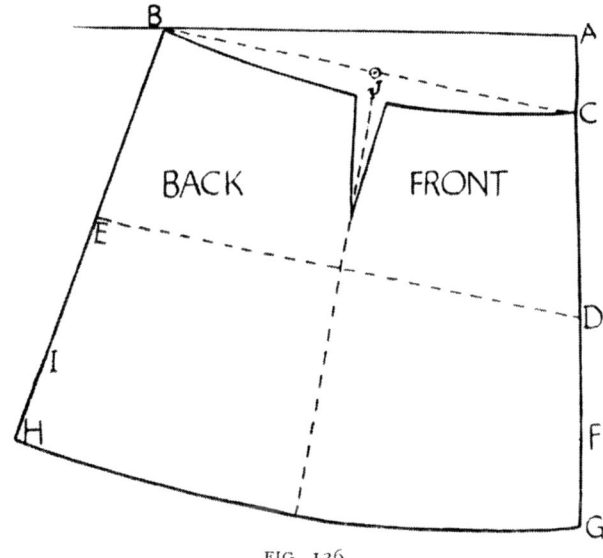

FIG. 136

that the draft so far resembles a skirt, and if extended to the required length would make a perfect fitting skirt or waist petticoat. (See Fig. 154.)

Fig. 137 shows the completed draft. Continuing from Fig. 136 square out from F one-sixth of line ED (note if wider legs are required plus ½ to 1 inch). Measure in ½ inch to ¾ inch from C and draw front body line through D and on to L as shown (Fig. 137).

GM = FL plus ½ inch. Square out from I.
IN = FL plus 2 inches.
HO = GM plus 2 inches. Measure in from B, ½ inch to ¾ inch and draw back body line through a point midway BE and on to N as shown in Fig. 137.

The pattern may be cut out in one piece as drafted, thus dispensing with side seams. Openings are made at each side fastening with buttons and buttonholes.

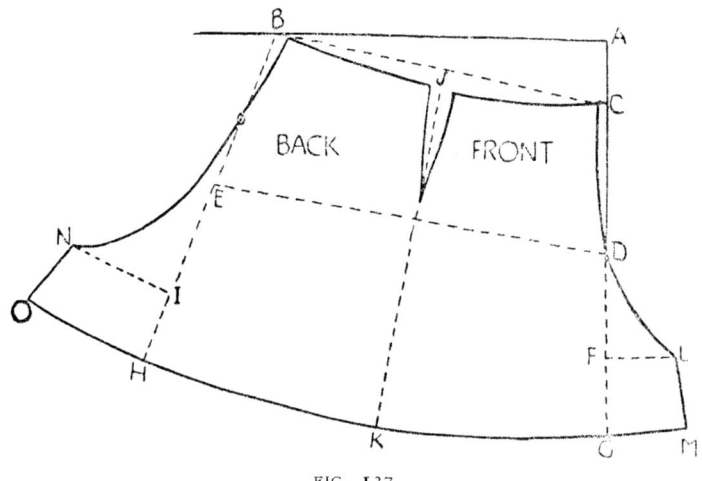

FIG. 137

KNICKER TYPE PATTERN

KNICKERS WITH PLEATS (Fig. 138). (Cut from skirt knickers pattern)

Pleated knickers are growing in favour with the woman who is not so slim as she would wish to be. The pleats give fullness and allow freedom of movement without bulkiness. The number of pleats is a matter of taste and weight of material to be used.

THE PATTERN

1. Cut the knicker pattern along the side seam and outline front and back sections on to paper.
2. Divide waist line of each section into thirds and rule dotted lines as shown for front (Fig. 139).
3. Cut on the dotted lines after numbering each piece.
4. Pin pieces of pattern on to paper separating each cut edge about 2 inches for the pleat allowance, and outline in this position (Fig. 140).
5. Add on to the side front pattern a wrap 2 inches wide and 8 inches deep. Add on to the side back pattern a wrap $2\frac{1}{2}$ inches wide and 8 inches deep.

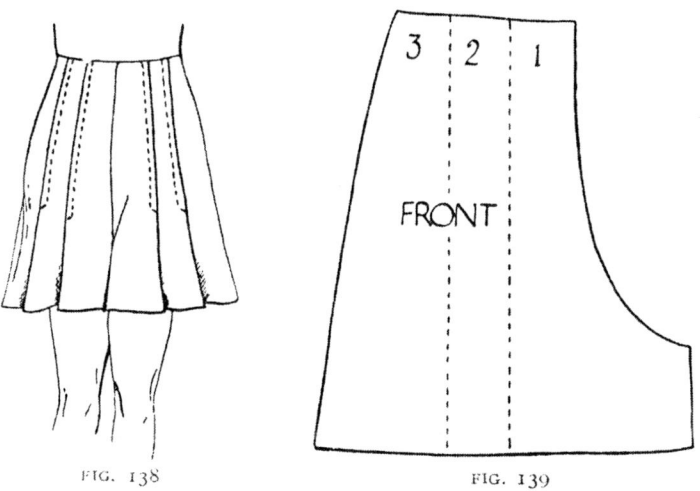

FIG. 138   FIG. 139

126 GERTRUDE MASON'S PATTERN BOOK

6. Transfer with tracing wheel the position and allowance for the pleats, and then cut out the new outline.

7. When pleating the material pleat on the solid lines and bring to traced lines (dotted) (Fig. 141).

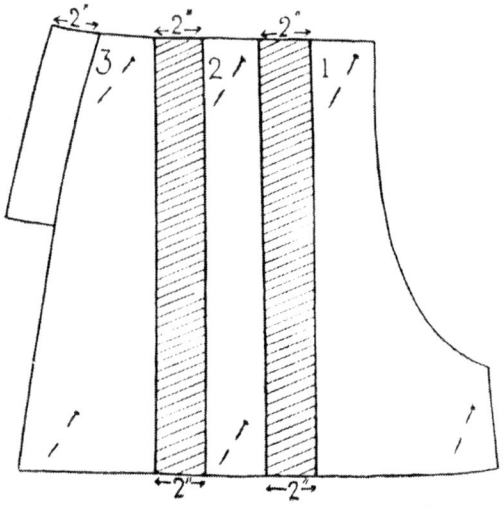

FIG. 140

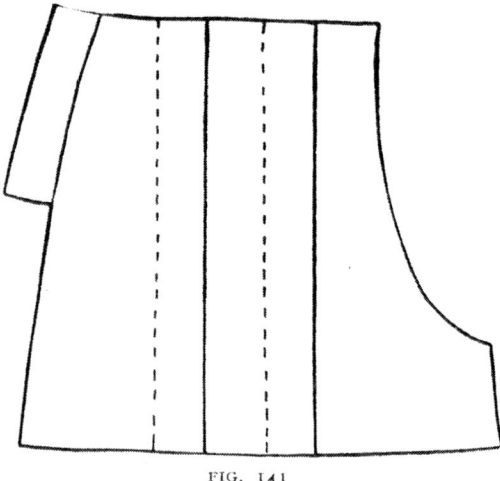

FIG. 141

KNICKER TYPE PATTERN

The same pattern can be used for pleated shorts and, when attached to a bodice, make an ideal sports suit for tennis or badminton.

TROUSER SKIRT (Fig. 142). (Cut from skirt knicker pattern)

This type of garment is provided with an inverted pleat back and front, to give freedom of movement, and to conceal the fork.

THE PATTERN, FIG. 143

1. Extend knicker pattern below fork line to length required as indicated by dotted line.

2. Cut the lengthened pattern down centre front line and separate the cut edges 8 inches (more or less) for the pleat allowance. Outline in this position on to paper and cut out. Adapt the back in a similar manner.

FIG. 142

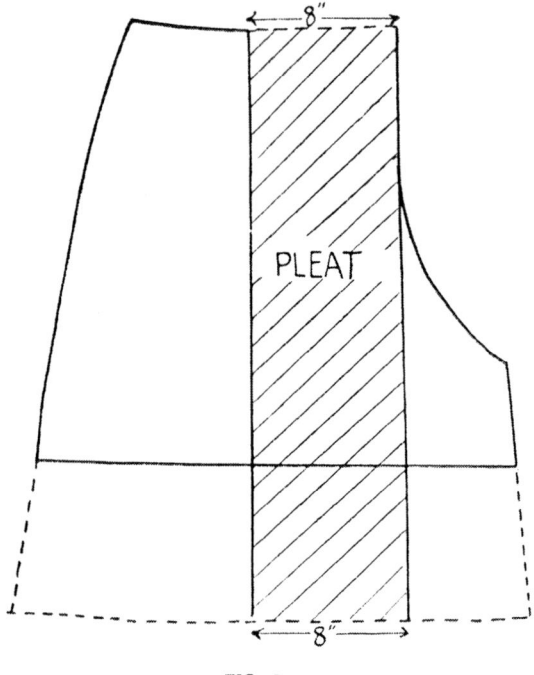

FIG. 143

VIII

SKIRT TYPE PATTERN

THE art of skirt cutting lies in the fitting of the hips and the balance of a skirt pattern depends upon the hip measurement. Accuracy in taking this measurement is therefore essential. Fig. 144 illustrates the draft of a two-piece skirt of the style worn by the figure (Fig. 66) on page 61.

To draft the skirt pattern (Fig. 144)

A large sheet of cutting out or brown paper will be required, also a long rule, tailor's chalk or pencil. The draft has been drawn to the following measurements :—Waist 28 inches. Hips 40 inches. Hem width 54 inches. Front length 31 inches. Side length 32 inches. Back length $31\frac{1}{2}$ inches.

Construction lines

First rule two lines at right angles and letter the corner A. B is $\frac{1}{6}$ of half the waist measure minus one inch from A.

Note—For a skirt measuring :—
- (a) 60 inches round the hem AB = $\frac{1}{6}$ of half the waist measure.
- (b) 72 inches round the hem AB = $\frac{1}{6}$ of half the waist measure plus 1 inch.

The width of the hem regulates the waist and the dip at the front.

C is eight inches down from B. Draw a dotted line across.

C-D is half the hip measure plus 1 inch (more or less).

E is the front length measure from B. Draw a dotted line across.

EF is half the width of the skirt. Place a ruler on F and D and rule to the waist construction line. This marks point G.

PATTERN LINES

Curve from B to G for the waist line. C to D^2 is the hip line, and parallel with the waist curve.

G-F^2 is the back length measure. Connect to E with a temporary line. Find the middle of the waist and hip lines and rule a dotted line to the hem line. H-I is the side length measure. Curve for the bottom of the skirt from E through I

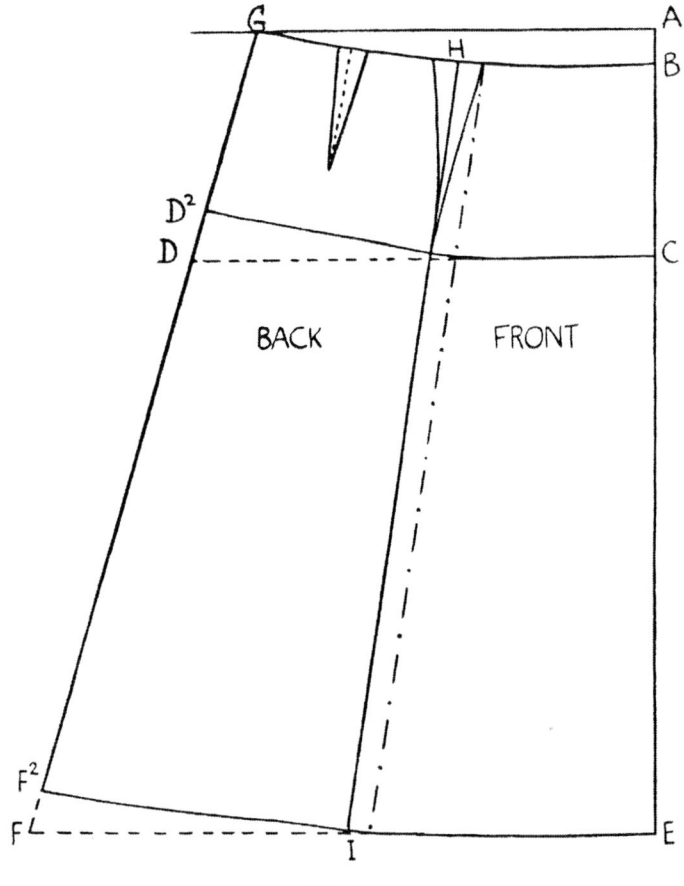

FIG. 144

SKIRT TYPE PATTERN

and on to F^2, keeping straight at E. The side seam, H-I may be moved forward 1 inch as suggested by dot and dash lines.

For the waist suppression

Measure waist line B-G. Add on half an inch to the half waist measurement ($14\frac{1}{2}$ inches) and subtract this from the measurement of the skirt waist line. The difference is the amount to be suppressed at the side seam and by a dart placed between side seam and centre of back as shown (Fig. 144).

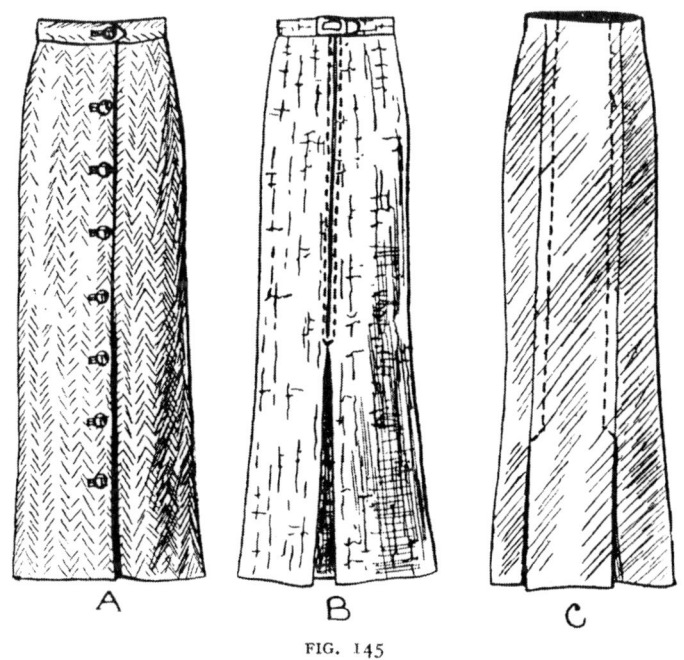

FIG. 145

ADAPTATIONS OF THE SKIRT PATTERN

The foundation skirt (Fig. 144) can be used for the three different styles of skirt illustrated (Fig. 145, A, B and C). Skirt A has a moderate overlap where holes and buttons are placed for fastening purposes. Style B is made with a seam and pleat centre front, while Style C has a knife pleat arranged each side of the centre front. To produce these skirts, first determine the amount of overlap required for skirt A and pleat allowance for skirts B and C. Add on this amount to the centre front of skirt pattern, and cut out as shown (Fig. 146). Fig. 147 (a) suggests how this extension

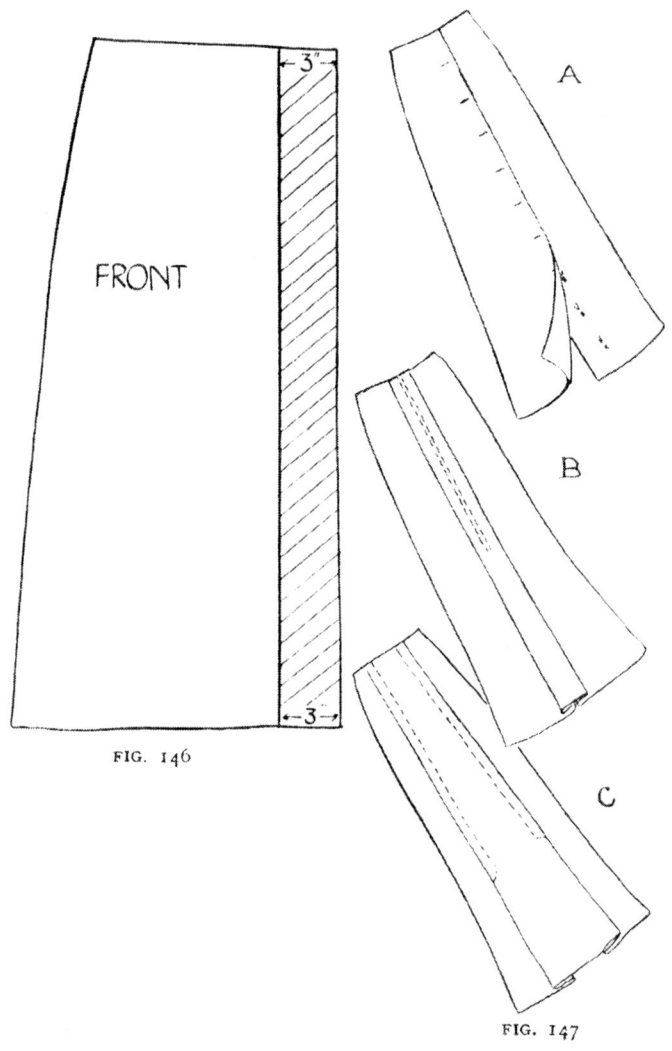

FIG. 146

FIG. 147

is arranged to form the wrap over. Both edges must be lined. The wrong side of the stitched inverted pleat is shown at (b), where it forms a box pleat. Fig. 147 (c) shows the front of Style C.

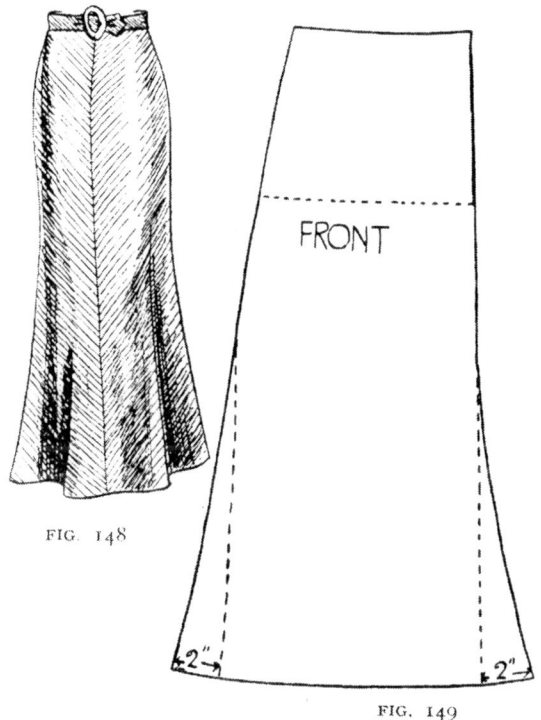

FIG. 148

FIG. 149

SKIRT WITH FLARES (Fig. 148)

This skirt has four seams with a moderate amount of flare at hem line. Fig. 149 shows the alteration of foundation pattern for flares; 2 inches is added at each seam. This principle is used for cami-knickers, page 122.

Another method of increasing the width of the hem line is as follows. Cut up the foundation pattern into three or four pieces. Pin centre front pattern to a perpendicular edge of paper and place the others in order with the hip line touching and open at the bottom to the required width. This will cause the pattern to overlap on the waist line. Re-draw the waist curve and test its measurement. This principle is illustrated in cutting circular knickers (Fig. 135). The foundation pattern can also be divided into three, four or six pieces, or gores,

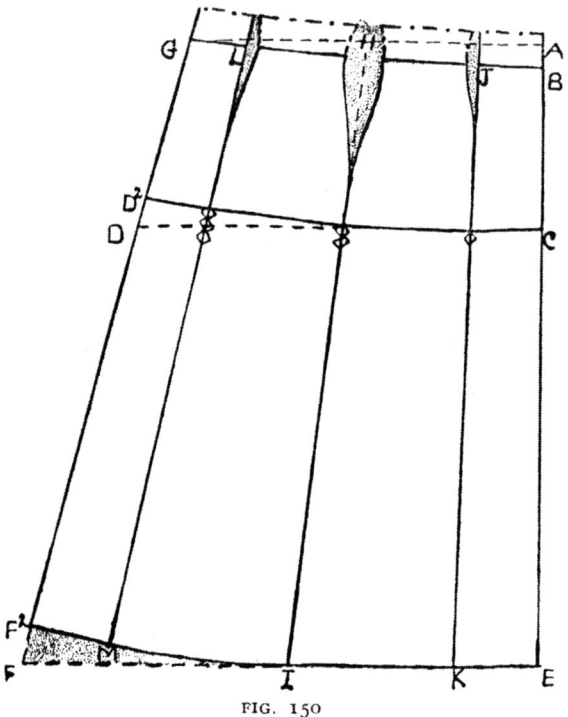

FIG. 150

according to fashion or requirements. Fig. 150 shows the skirt pattern divided into 4 gores. To divide for the gores, determine the size of the front panel. This depends on the width of the skirt and the demands of fashion. The width of the front panel BJ (Fig. 150) is $3\frac{1}{4}$ inches. EK is $4\frac{1}{4}$ inches. *Note*—with wider skirts the panel may measure at the hem line from one and a half to two and a half times its size at the waist, see panel petticoat (Fig. 48) page 45.

SKIRT TYPE PATTERN 135

Make back panel G-L and F²M (Fig. 150) similar in size to the front. The difference between the half waist measurement and the half skirt waist line measurement is now suppressed at the panel and side seams. When the skirt is drafted, notch the hip line as shown so that no mistake shall be made when putting together.

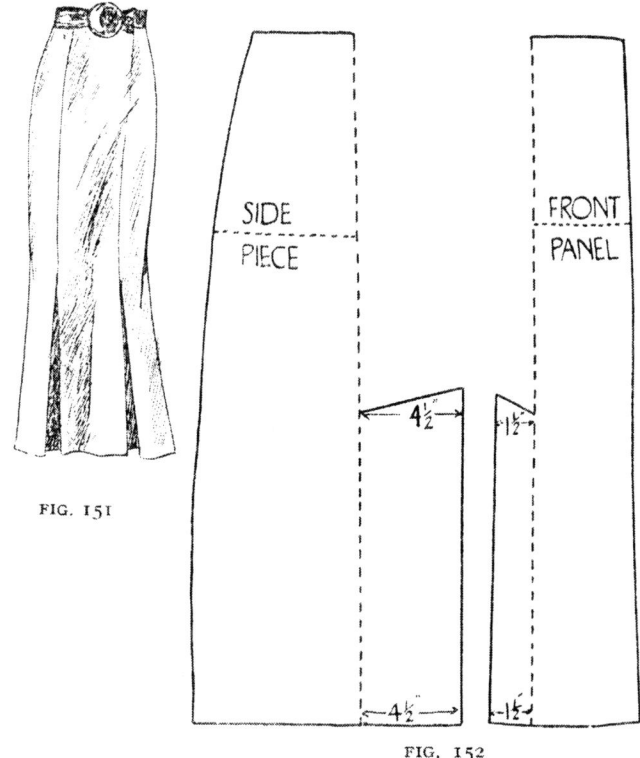

FIG. 151

FIG. 152

A PANEL PLEATED SKIRT (Fig. 151)

Inverted pleats are added to the front panel of this skirt. First determine the size of pleat required then add a quarter to one side of the seam, and three times this amount at the other as shown (Fig. 152). This arrangement prevents the

K

seam from falling midway between the pleat where it would be most conspicuous. The pleat is usually about 14 inches up from hem line.

A SIX-GORED SKIRT (Fig. 153)

This is a very graceful skirt, particularly suitable for dancing or skating as illustrated ; the length, of course, depending on taste and circumstances. For this skirt it is advisable to draft a pattern measuring 72 inches round the hem. Refer to pages 133 & 134. As fashion alters so much in respect to fullness it may be necessary to cut it of ample dimensions. If this is the case make BC $\frac{1}{6}$ of half waist plus 2 or 3 inches. After drafting the foundation determine the size of the gores. This depends on the width of the skirt, fashion and personal preference. Make the width of the gore at the hem twice, or two and a half times that at the waist. This pattern may be utilised for the tunic illustrated, Fig. 161. Use the two-piece foundation pattern for the underskirt.

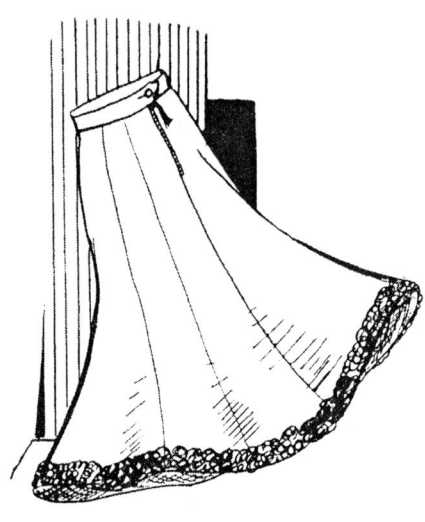

FIG. 153

A WAIST OR SKIRT PETTICOAT (Fig. 154)

A petticoat from the waist is very useful for wear under a thin dress, which perhaps already has its own slip, but which is still not shadow proof.

Unlined dresses and skirts made of modern woollen and

mixture materials call for well-fitting underskirts as a foundation to avoid that tendency to cling to the figure which is characteristic of these fabrics.

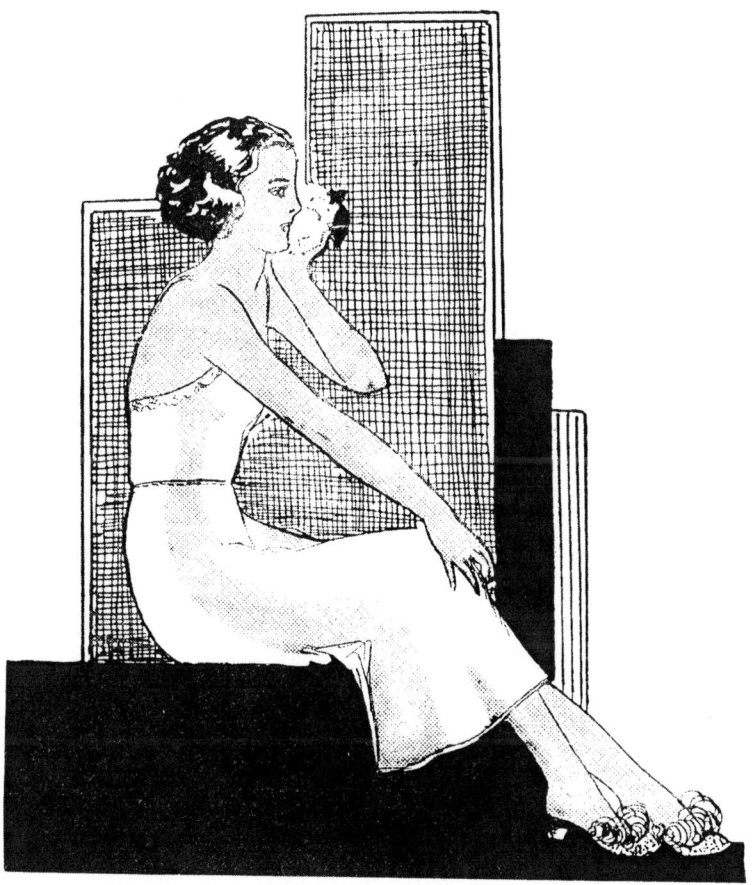

FIG. 154

SKIRT PETTICOAT (Fig. 155A)

A may be cut from the two-piece skirt pattern or from the lower part of the one-piece foundation (Fig. 107). A pleated godet is inserted at centre front of skirt to provide extra

138 GERTRUDE MASON'S PATTERN BOOK

hem width. For method of obtaining the yoke for B, refer to Fig. 130, page 118.

PATTERN OF THE GODET (Fig. 156)

Measure up from lower edge of skirt the required length of godet (12 inches to 14 inches). Take paper, fold it, and mark

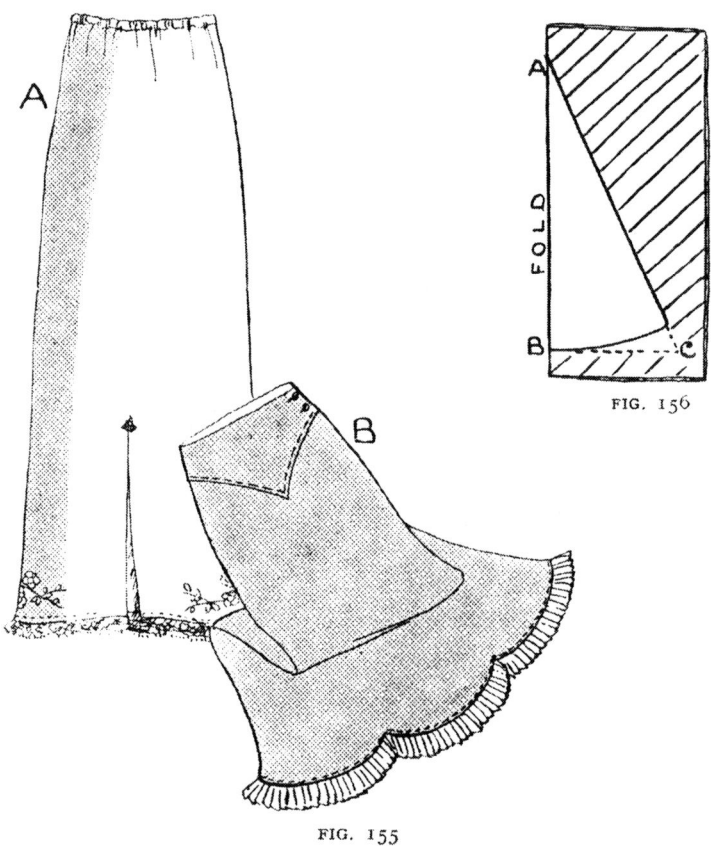

FIG. 155

FIG. 156

the length of godet AB on the folded edge. BC is half the required width (8 to 10 inches). Rule dotted line AC and make AC the same length as AB. Complete as shown (Fig. 156).

USES OF THE GODET

Fullness and slimness are sometimes required in a garment, particularly in the case of evening and dance frocks. It is only by means of the godet that this effect can be achieved. The godet may be inserted at each side of a dress from the hip line, or the narrowest of skirts, or foundation patterns can be made voluminous by inserting a series of godets.

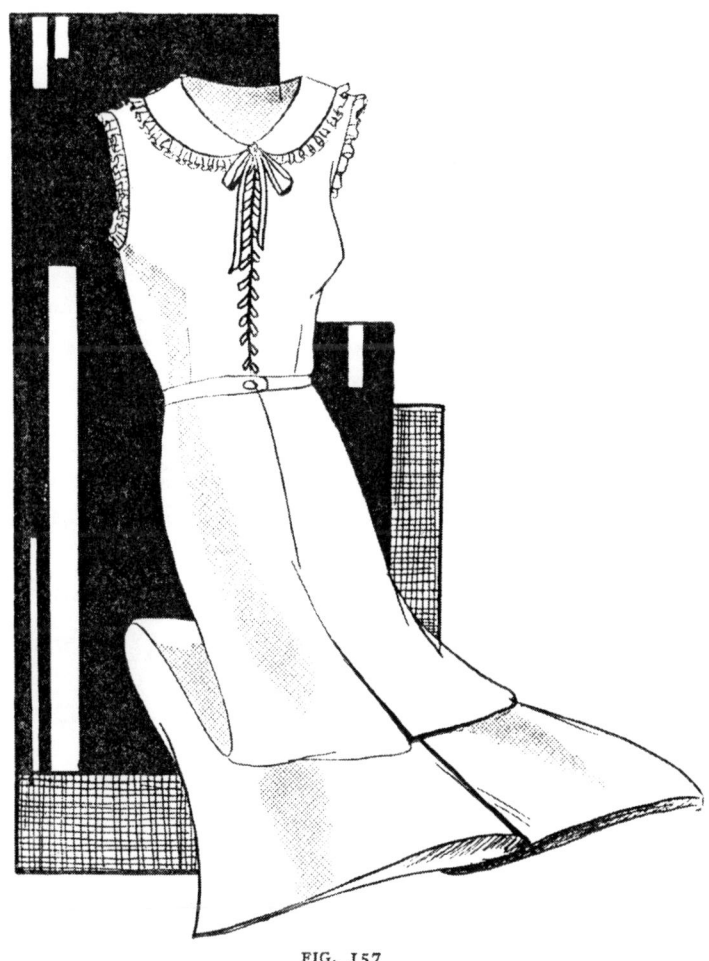

FIG. 157

MODERN COMBINED GARMENTS

With the marked change in the cut and fashion of clothes has come the necessity to reduce the number of undergarments worn. There is a strong tendency also to combine two garments into one. Cami-knickers have already been referred to as a neat, serviceable and economical combination of camisole and knickers.

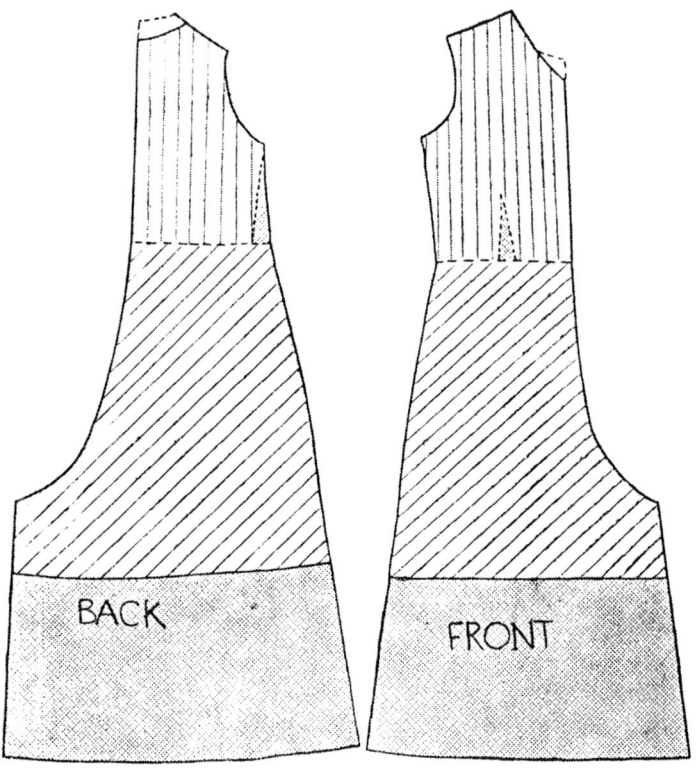

FIG. 158

ALL-IN-ONE PYJAMAS (Fig. 157)

A combination of bodice pattern (Fig. 68) and skirt knicker pattern (Fig. 137).

SKIRT TYPE PATTERN 141

THE PATTERN, FIG. 158

Required. A bodice and skirt knicker pattern to fit the wearer.

Pin patterns on to paper as clearly shown (Fig 158), and

FIG. 159

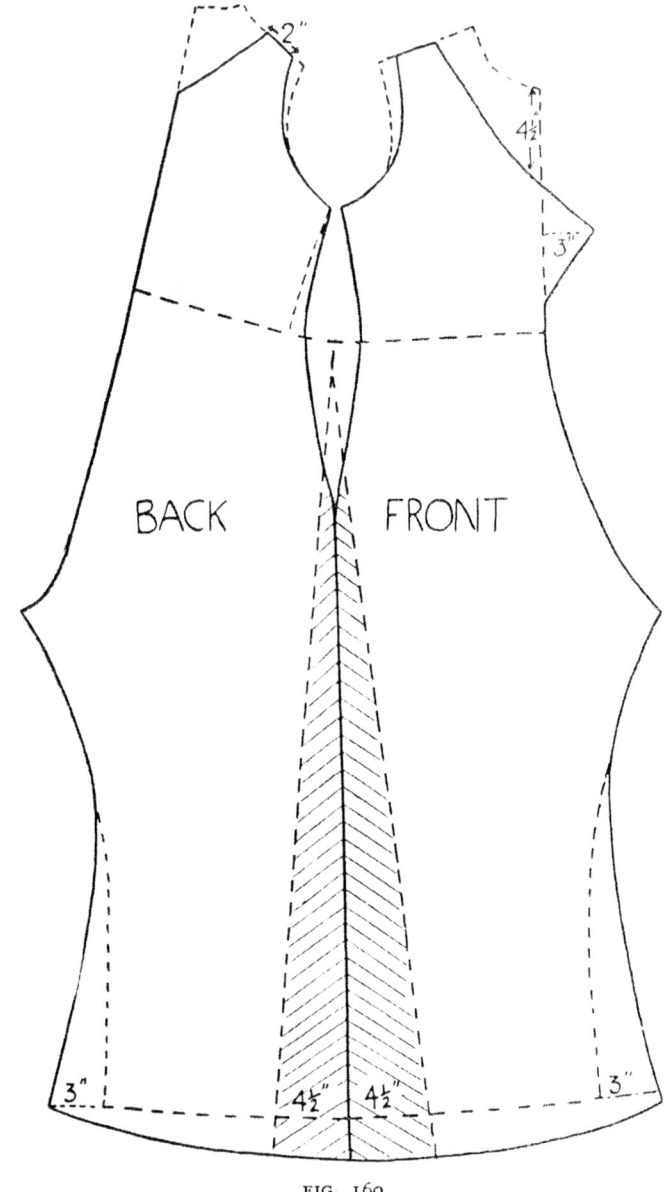

FIG. 160

SKIRT TYPE PATTERN

make the back waist line of bodice the same measurement as the knicker waist line. Re-shape back side seam. Adapt neck curve as desired. Extend the knickers from waist to ankle the required side length measure, as indicated by shading (Fig. 158). Complete the pattern and cut out along the altered lines.

PYJAMA NIGHTDRESS (Fig. 159)

The old combinations pattern still survives and a very modern interpretation of it is shown in this nightdress.

THE PATTERN, FIG. 160

Required. Bodice and pyjama trouser pattern to fit the wearer.

Rule a perpendicular line on to a sheet of paper. Cut down the side seam of the trouser pattern and separate the cut edges $4\frac{1}{2}$ inches each side the perpendicular line as shown (Fig. 160). Note that the edges meet at the waist line. Place the waist

FIG. 161

lines of back and front bodice pattern to the trouser waist line and outline. Remove block patterns, re-shape side lines, and adapt bodice as Fig. 160. Measure out 3 inches at lower edge of pattern, add on 2½ to 3 inches of round at side line and shape hem line as shown (Fig. 160).

Cut out along the altered pattern lines. The tunic dress (Fig. 161) is a combination of several patterns already referred to on previous pages. (a) Bodice with ornamental darts (Fig. 70). (b) Sleeve with fullness (Fig. 81). (c) Stand collar (Fig. 89). (d) Tunic skirt, either Fig. 149 or Fig. 153, and (e) underskirt (Fig. 144). It has only been possible to give a few patterns of combined garments and if space permitted, many other arrangements might be described. If changes are made with bodice, sleeve, collar and skirt patterns, several patterns in different styles can be produced.

From the numerous examples and explanations of pattern making given in this book, the reader will see how easy it is to reduce the apparent intricacies of any model to its elements, and evolve almost any design she pleases.

The principles of pattern cutting applied to coats will be found in *Tailoring for Women*.

TESTING THE PAPER PATTERN

Before cutting out in material, it is advisable to test the pattern on the figure to be assured that it is satisfactory. To do this, gum or pin together at intervals the shoulder and underarm seams to 1 inch wide strips of paper. Slip on the paper pattern and note what alterations (if any) are required. Remove the pattern, and then take the pattern pieces apart. Lay them flat on a table and with ruler and pencil make any necessary adjustments.

CUTTING OUT THE PAPER PATTERN IN MATERIAL

The pattern is now ready to be pinned on to the material and cut out, but before this process can be attempted it is necessary to consider the "way" of the material, and also prepare it for cutting.

THE WAY OF THE MATERIAL

All woven materials are composed of two sets of threads, lengthway threads, and widthway threads, technically called warp and weft. In process of manufacture the warp or selvedge threads are stretched and twisted and made a certain strength as these threads have to bear most weight and strain in wear. The weft threads are woven in and out of the selvedge threads and are weaker and looser, therefore the widthway of materials stretches more than the selvedge way. Every woman who sews should understand the material grains, as half the success of cutting out is assured by having each piece of the pattern cut with the grain of the material running exactly in the right direction, straight up and down, straight across, or on the exact cross. The general rule in cutting out garments is that all parts of the pattern should be placed on the material with the warp threads running from top to bottom. There are exceptions to this rule as certain parts of garments such as yokes, collars, cuffs, etc., which have to bear the greatest strain in wear should be so arranged that the warp or strongest threads run round, not down the figure. Sometimes fashion overrides these rules for the warp, or selvedge threads, and decrees that garments shall be cut on the crossway threads of the material to give them that elastic moulding which will make them fit smoothly. All garments cut on this modern principle fall in subtle clinging lines of their own accord and "give" to the wearer's movements without any strain on the material, and thus last so much longer. Flounces, folds, facings, and bindings are usually cut on the cross because material is always more pliable cut this way, and can be readily shaped to fit curves, etc.

Preparation of material for cutting

All double width materials have a firmly marked crease running lengthways in the centre of their width. In nearly all materials there are to be found irregular creases due to careless folding, or handling. Creases should always be removed with a hot iron before cutting out is begun. Frequently this is neglected because it takes time but those who do it find themselves repaid. Before laying the pattern on the material, both the ends of the material should be on a perfectly straight grain.

Folding material for cutting

As paper patterns are cut for one half of the figure only, each part should be cut in double material whenever possible to avoid confusion. Sometimes it is advisable to open out the material and refold it across its width, wide enough to take the largest piece of pattern, thus leaving a single strip of material. When cutting knickers it is usual to fold the material weft way, using the whole width or nearly the whole width for the pattern.

To cut garments on the cross, open out the material single width and mark off with a pin on one selvedge a length exactly equal to the width of the material. Fold over one corner till it exactly meets the opposite selvedge, forming a triangle. The line at the fold running diagonally across the warp and weft threads is the true cross of the material. Press the fold lightly, just sufficiently to act as a guide.

PLANNING OUT THE PATTERN

Planning out the pattern to the best advantage with the greatest economy of material is a very interesting one and it is pleasing to discover how by ingenuity a garment may be cut from a much smaller quantity than was anticipated. But though economy should be aimed at, the " grain " of the material should be the first consideration. Having found the grain of the material and refolded it for the sake of economy, place each piece of the pattern so that this grain is running in its right direction, straight up and down, straight across or on the exact cross.

Where a straight edge of the pattern is placed to a fold, see that the pattern actually touches the fold. Obtain and place all parts of the pattern on the material before commencing to cut round any one. Use fine steel pins and pin the pattern through both layers of the material at the corners and round the curves. Pin at right angles to the edge of the pattern. Leave room between the pieces of pattern for the seam allowance which is marked off outside the edge of the paper pattern with pins, pencil, tailors' chalk, or tracing wheel according to the texture of the material. Make the following allowances for seams :

Shoulder and underarm seams	½ to 1 inch.
Armhole	¼ inch.
Neck and collar edges	¼ to ½ inch.
Sleeve seams	½ inch.

Needlewomen should endeavour to cultivate ability to judge small distances accurately and to cut evenly with exactly the required allowance for seams. If this is done it is not always necessary to mark out the cutting line, as the " fitting " line is bound to be at a distance from the edge equal to the seam allowance allowed. Mark the outline of each piece of pattern with a tracing wheel, or tailors' tacks or press back the seam allowance over the pattern with a warm iron, according to the thickness and texture of the material. With some modern materials it is advisable to trace the outline of each section of the pattern and cut as few sections as possible for making up, and then of those sections only the seams that are to be worked on immediately. A neck line should not be cut until the first fitting.

THE CUTTING OUT

Cutting out is a very important branch of the needlewoman's art. Many adults cut out badly and jagged edges, uneven seams, and failure to fit are the result. To be a good cutter-out requires a knowledge of certain rules, great practice, and an infinite power of contrivance.

It is essential that the scissors should be used correctly in order to ensure clean cut edges to the material. It is the cutting out which makes or mars the contour line. It will be noticed that the end of one blade is narrow, while that of the other is broad. The handle from the narrow end has a hole to fit the thumb and that from the broad end has, as a rule, a wider one to fit two fingers. The scissors should be held in the right hand with the broad blade uppermost whilst the narrow one moves under the material, practically resting on the table as it goes along, so that the whole blade is used. The blades should be opened as widely as possible and then closed very smartly, to avoid a jerky series of snips. When the blades are closed a grating noise is produced, which is a correct accompaniment to good cutting.

The bulk of the pattern should be kept to the left-hand side when cutting out so that the scissors can be used at the right-hand edges. The fingers and palm of the left hand should be laid upon the pattern so that a firmness is given. The material must be kept flat upon the table and only raised from it just as much as is necessary to insert the scissors blade under it.